THE MANY LIVES OF
ANDREW CARNEGIE

THE MANY LIVES OF
ANDREW CARNEGIE

Milton Meltzer

FRANKLIN WATTS
A Division of Grolier Publishing
New York London Hong Kong Sydney
Danbury, Connecticut

Photographs ©:Photographs ©:Brown Brothers: 28, 52, 62, 71, 92, 99, 117, 140; Courtesy of Carnegie Corporation Archive: 93, 131; Carnegie Library of Pittsburgh: 14, 22, 56, 75 right, 75 left, 127, 132, 135; Corbis-Bettmann: 49, 61, 66, 109, 123; Culver Pictures: 16, 24, 37, 68, 73, 75 middle, 79, 147; Milton Meltzer: 142; Museum of the City of New York: 59; New York Public Library Picture Collection: 137; New York Public Library, Rare Book Division: 120; North Wind Picture Archives: 97, 101.

Library of Congress Cataloging-in-Publication Data

Meltzer, Milton, 1915–
    The many lives of Andrew Carnegie / Milton Meltzer
        p. cm. —(Milton Meltzer biographies)
    Includes biographical references and index.
    Summary: A biography of the Scottish immigrant who made a fortune in the steel industry and used much of it for philanthropic causes.
    ISBN 0-531-11427-9
    1. Carnegie, Andrew, 1835–1919. 2. Industrialists—United — States—Biography. —Philanthropists—United States—Biography.
    [1. Carnegie, Andrew, 1835 -1919. 2. Industrialists.
    3. Philanthropists.] I. Title. II. Series: Meltzer, Milton, 1915– Milton Meltzer Biographies.
    CT275.C3M38. 1997
    338.7'672'092—dc21
    [B]   96-40144
                                           CIP
                                         AC

CONTENTS

FOREWORD

When I was growing up in Worcester, Massachusetts, I loved to read Horatio Alger's stories: *Sink or Swim, Strive and Succeed, Wait and Hope, Pluck and Luck*. These short paperback books really had only one story to tell. The hero is a poor but honest boy (like me) and usually an orphan (not like me). He has to make it on his own, so he goes off to the big city. After a string of exciting adventures, the young hero saves the life of a rich man's daughter. Her grateful father gives the boy a job in his business, and soon the climb from rags to riches is on its way. The young hero is bright and eager. He always does the right thing, proves his good character, and wins a high place in the world because he deserves it.

I believed in the truth of Alger's stories, even though I never met anyone who had risen from rags to riches. Rags, I knew—the clean ones my father used to wash the windows by which he made our family's living. But riches?

Still, I read in the Sunday paper now and then of real people who were like Alger's heroes—Cornelius Vanderbilt, John D. Rockefeller, Henry Ford, and others who made a dazzling gallery of success-gods. So maybe we too, the children of working-class immigrant families, could win fame and fortune one day.

Maybe we could do it just the way Andrew Carnegie had done.

I had heard extraordinary things about that man. Maybe you have too. And like you, I wanted to find out more. (That's how this book got started.)

For instance:

Andy was born dirt-poor in a small town in Scotland but made himself the richest man in the *world*.

He had only five years of elementary schooling but would write scores of articles and many books and become a close friend of many leading statesmen and writers.

He loved books so much he wanted everyone to have access to them. You can scarcely find a town or city in the United States that doesn't have a public library built with Carnegie's money. He paid for nearly three thousand of them, worldwide.

When he was only 33, Carnegie was already so rich that it disgusted him. He said the worship of money, which he saw all around him, was degrading. He resolved to quit business soon and devote himself to making life better for all. Soon? He kept making more and more money for another 30 years before he retired.

He hated war but his steel mills made armor plate for the battleships of many nations.

As a boy in Scotland, Andy was raised by a family of radicals he proudly said risked everything to fight against the powerful for freedom, justice, and equality for all. Yet this man built a colossal steel industry, employed tens of thousands of workers, but never paid them a living wage.

Andy preached to the world that "the right of workingmen to form trade unions is 'sacred,'" and yet he approved the bloody crushing of a strike for higher wages in his steel mills.

Andy's childhood was spent in a two-room stone cottage in Dunfermline, Scotland. Years later, he returned to Scotland to build himself a castle as large and luxurious as any king had ever owned.

What kind of man was this?

What made him what he was?

What meaning does such a life have for us today?

ONE

RADICAL
TO THE CORE

One of Andy's earliest memories was of being awakened during the night by a tapping at the back window. Men stood out on the street calling up to his parents that Andy's uncle Bailie Morrison had been thrown into jail.

Why? Because he had dared to hold a protest rally that the authorities had forbidden.

It was the 1840s, when the people of Britain were agitating for repeal of laws Parliament had adopted that did great harm to workers and farmers. All the men in the Carnegie family—father, grandfathers, uncles—were radicals who never feared to demonstrate for their rights. There had been riots in the town, and a troop of cavalry was sent in to break up the demonstrations. Now as Andy's uncle was being escorted to jail an immense crowd followed the sheriff's men, hooting and jeering, bent on rescuing their leader.

But Andy's uncle, like all in the family, did not believe in using force and violence. He went to the jail window and urged the crowd to go home peacefully. Moral force, not physical force, will prevail, he said.

Everyone in the Carnegie family was "radical to the core," Andy would proudly recall years later. They hated Britain's monarchy and its system where aristocrats and wealthy landlords made laws for their own enrichment. Look at America, they said, it's different there. The people admired the way the young American republic did things, and these beliefs were helped along by many Dunfermliners who had already crossed the Atlantic to seek a better life. Why couldn't Britain become a democratic society where people were free and equal?

It was on such ideas that young Andy was raised. "As a child," he said, "I could have slain king, duke or lord, and considered their death a service to the state and hence a heroic act." The village of Dunfermline, Scotland, where Andy was born on the cold and wet day of November 25, 1835, was famous as a center of revolutionary ferment. William Carnegie, Andy's father, was a regular speaker at political rallies, which happened almost daily during the 1840s. And that jailed uncle, Bailie Morrison, was a passionate orator for the rights of the working class to vote and to strike. "It is not to be wondered at," wrote Carnegie, "that, nursed amid such surroundings, I developed into a violent young Republican whose motto was 'death to privilege.'"

Dunfermline was a one-industry town when Andy was born. Linen weaving was the heart of its economic life. Of some 12,000 townfolk, almost half—men, women, and children—worked in the linen weaving industry. It was an ancient trade, with weavers listed in the town records as far back as the time Columbus sailed for America. By 1835, most of the looms in town were weaving damask, a fine linen, creating wonderful designs of fruits and flowers.

Weavers like Andy's father were proud of their artistry. William Carnegie's family had been skilled weavers for generations. And Margaret Carnegie's family, the Morrisons, had handcrafted shoes for just as many generations. They rated themselves as high in craftsmanship as goldsmiths, jewelers, and cabinetmakers. Not for them were the grimy lives of the coal miners in neighboring towns, or the cotton mill workers who slaved at their machines in Lanarkshire and Manchester.

But the family's crafts were already in danger. The shift to machine production—the industrial revolution—that began in England was replacing animals, windmills, waterwheels, and men as sources of power for manufacturing. Steam boilers, run on England's plentiful supply of coal, unleashed a new source of enormous energy. It could multiply by unbelievable numbers the output of old industry and open new fields to profitable investment.

Would industrialization mean the end of the poverty and unemployment that had cursed Britain for so long? Some expected it would; many hoped so. Yet in Dunfermline new inventions threatened to wipe out the trades of artisans in many fields. Great power looms had invaded the spinning and weaving of cotton. By the time of Andy's birth the hand-loom weavers of cotton had been forced to give up their craft. To survive, they, with their wives and children, had to beg for work in the new mills. Their earnings dropped dramatically.

And now the linen industry, too, was being industrialized. The introduction of new power looms revolutionized the weaving of damask. The Carnegie family's pride in their artistry, in their ancient and honorable craft, began to crumble under the relentless pressure of the industrial revolution.

Andy's birthplace was a small stone cottage that served the family as both home and workshop. Mr. Carnegie's hand loom was on the ground floor. The tiny attic above had to do for the family's living quarters. As the first-born son, the infant was named Andrew after his paternal grandfather. The healthy infant, everyone noticed, had an unusually large head.

The weaver's cottage in Dunfermline, Scotland, where Andrew Carnegie was born in 1835

Grandpa Andrew was a popular character in the district, known for his wit and humor. "A brainy man," people said, who read widely and thought for himself. He became leader of the radical weavers of Dunfermline. They formed a club and called their meeting place "Patiemuir College," dubbing Andy's grandpa "Professor." His grandson often said he owed his optimistic nature, his ability to shed his troubles and laugh, to his delightful old grandfather.

On his mother's side, Andy's grandfather, Thomas Morrison, was esteemed as a great organizer. He built his radical group around a program of political action and nonviolent resistance. He edited a radical newspaper that strongly promoted a technical education for young people. "I thank God," he wrote, "that in my youth I learned to make and mend shoes." (It was that grandfather's son, Bailie, who went to jail.)

Long after, when the local folk saw Andrew Carnegie after a lapse of many years, they remarked on his astonishing likeness to that grandfather. He not only looked like him but even gestured like him.

Andy would later say that his mother, Margaret, was "my favorite heroine." She was a dignified, refined little woman whom he adored. She had blonde hair and eyes, a strong jaw and determined chin. Her iron will and intense loyalty to family would do much to shape Andy's future. But he never, in all his writings, could bring himself to say much about his mother. After his father's early death, she became "all my own," he wrote.

Just as he took pride in his ancestors, so Andy felt lucky in his birthplace. He knew that where you're born and brought up—the surroundings, the traditions, the history—can greatly influence what becomes of you. Dunfermline could boast of the ruins of a great monastery and of a palace where kings had been born. The tomb of the Scottish hero Robert the Bruce was in the center of the great abbey. Andy saw Dunfermline as a romantic town, standing on high ground, overlooking the sea, with Edinburgh in view to the south and a mountain range to the north. It made him conscious of "the mighty past when Dunfermline was both nationally and religiously the capital of Scotland."

In the early years of Andy's life his father did well enough in the weaving business for the family to move to a larger house. Four weaving looms, run with the help of apprentices, occupied the lower floor while the family lived upstairs. Mr. Carnegie, like the other linen weavers, was a small businessman, owning his own looms. He did not keep regular hours. Instead, he worked whenever the larger manufacturers sent him material to be woven.

By the time Andy was four he was exploring the world outside his home. He toddled along the cobbled streets of Dunfermline, looking into the loom shops of other weavers, sniffing the catch in the fish market, feeling the

Handloom weaving, the craft by which Carnegie's father made his living.

fabrics in the draper shops, and pestering Uncle Tom in his leather shop.

Beyond the town spread the green fields where linen was hung up to bleach in the sun, and a boy could leap high to grab onto the wooden bars that held the linen up and go swinging into the sky.

In summer Andy might listen to the preachers voices coming out of their tents encouraging the faithful to do good works. Monthly trade fairs brought in a rich variety of goods for Andy to examine, and maybe he could coax an apple out of a fruit seller or a cookie out of a baker.

But the most exciting time for young Andy was New Year's Eve (not Christmas, because the Protestant Scots ignored it as a Catholic holiday). Mrs. Carnegie would serve up a great dinner for the family and Pa's apprentices. After the meal, Andy would put on a costume and a mask he'd spent weeks creating and dash out into the street to join his pals. They knocked at door after door, clamoring for the traditional three-cornered biscuits. Then, as the darkness deepened, the children would go off to home and bed—but not to sleep. Now it was the grownups' time to celebrate. When the abbey's bells tolled in the new year, they sallied out into the streets, carrying blazing torches and knocking at doors to be greeted with a glass of whisky and a biscuit.

Andy's uncle George Lauder did much to develop in the boy a sense of history and of his own place in a changing world. Lauder had married Mrs. Carnegie's elder sister, who died young, leaving him with a small son, George Jr. Nicknamed "Dod," George Jr. played with "Naig," as Andy was called. They were often in Uncle George's grocery store, and when business was slow, he would fascinate them for hours with wondrous tales of history. Carnegie would remember those informal lessons gratefully:

> *My uncle possessed an extraordinary gift of dealing with children and taught us many things. . . . Among others I remember how he taught us British history by imagining each of the monarchs in a certain place upon the walls of the room performing the act for which he was well known. . . . It was from my uncle that I learned all that I know of the early history of Scotland—of Wallace and Bruce and Burns. . . . I can truly say in the words of Burns that there was then and there created in me a vein of Scottish prejudice (or patriotism) which will cease to exist only with life.*

It is a source of great strength when a youngster has a hero, and William Wallace (1272?–1305) was Andy's. He was a soldier who fought at the head of an army to oust the English from Scotland. Captured, he was executed. But Scottish resistance continued under Robert the Bruce (1274–1329), who gradually cleared the English out of most of Scotland. Robert Burns (1759–96), a farmer's son, wrote fresh and racy poems of rural life. His fiery lyrics for liberty and his songs ("My Heart's in the Highland" and "Auld Lang Syne" are but two of many) made him beloved by all.

It was Andy's mother who taught him the practical side of everyday living. She was in charge of family finances, she knew how every spare penny had to be put away, and she took care of the family garden.

Although she, too, like the rest of the family, gave her heart to the radical movement, she had no romantic expectation that tomorrow would bring a paradise on earth. Don't count on anyone to give you your daily bread, she would say to Andy; you eat only what you can buy with the money you earn through hard work. In the years to come Andy would demonstrate how deeply in him she had planted those roots.

Schooling for most Dunfermline children began at age five. But when Andy refused to go, his patient parents said that he didn't have to start until he was ready. One year, two years, three years passed with Andy living a free and easy life, and giving no sign he'd ever want to sit in a classroom. Desperate, his parents asked a neighboring schoolmaster, Robert Martin, to convince their boy school was a good thing—and fun. Mr. Martin took Andy on an excursion with some boys, and the next day Andy announced he'd go to Mr. Martin's school. He was then eight.

Britain had no free public education system at that time. Schools were private, charging fees to parents. Mr. Martin's was the cheapest, costing just a few pence a week. The only teacher, he crammed more than 150 children of all ages into one big room. Imagine trying to learn in such conditions! The older children listened to the younger ones recite and corrected their mistakes. But several groups recited all at once, and it sounded like a madhouse. The only thing that kept a minimum degree of order was Mr. Martin's leather whip. Despite that kind of discipline, Andy would remember Mr. Martin as "the first great man" he ever knew.

Andy proved to be an eager and talented student. He pushed himself to the utmost, as he always would in whatever he attempted, and stood out among the best. That earned him the label "teacher's pet." He shone especially in his mastery of poetry. He loved memorizing whole swatches of it. He earned his very first penny from Mr. Martin by a flawless and passionate recitation of a Robert Burns poem, "Man was Made to Mourn." Andy stoutly differed with Burns's message, though: man was not made to mourn but to make for himself a glorious future.

But he wanted this future not just for himself. With his radical upbringing, Andy dreamed of a good life for all. Material success for the individual was not his goal. Like his family he believed that once political equality was won, the people would use their democratic rights to create a happy and peaceful world.

POVERTY
AND DESPAIR

But "the good life for all" came to seem more and more only a dream. In the 1840s an economic depression gripped Britain. As it grew worse, unemployment increased. Jobless men and women roamed from town to town hunting for work. Along the roads of Scotland they slept in sheds or out in the open.

Hand-loom weavers had already tasted the bitterness of hard times. Their proud craft had been crippled by the introduction of steam-loom weaving. Mr. Carnegie could not face the revolutionary changeover and kept struggling vainly to make a go of it on the old craft system. But he got so little work that Andy's mother had to step in to keep the family afloat. She opened a small grocery shop, making barely enough to keep the family going. At night she stayed up stitching shoes by candlelight. Recalling that time, Andy wrote:

> I remember shortly after this I began to learn what poverty meant. Dreadful days came when my father took the last of his webs to the great manufacturer and I saw my

mother anxiously awaiting his return to know whether a new web was to be obtained or that a period of idleness was upon us. It was burnt into my heart that my father, though neither "abject, mean, nor vile," as Burns has it, had nevertheless to

"Beg a brother of the earth
To give him leave to toil."
And then and there came the resolve that I would cure that when I got to be a man.

Britain had become a land of great contrasts. It could boast of "the greatest accumulated wealth in history—and the worse slums in Christendom." Not only were there slums in the cities, but there was poverty and despair in the rural areas. Although Britain's empire extended to the far corners of the earth, it only made the rich richer and did nothing for anyone else.

It was no wonder that when *The Rights of Man* (1791), the fiery pamphlet written by Tom Paine, the hero of two revolutions, had circulated throughout Britain, its promise of liberty and equality ignited fierce passions. The cry for reform rose from millions of throats, and the Crown and Parliament had quaked in fear of revolution. Yet now, 50 years later, there had been little change for the better.

Factory workers in northern England and Scotland went on strike in 1842. By shutting down the mills they hoped to force the government to adopt remedial measures. Weavers, disguising themselves by soot-blackened faces, burned down a small power-loom mill. (That was when Andy's uncle was thrown into jail.) But with the aid of government troops the general strike was smashed.

The depression deepened. Even the families of highly skilled weavers suffered hunger. And with it came disease and death. Among the victims was Andy's younger sister, Ann. Then in 1843, Andy's brother, Tom, was born—anoth-

Andrew Carnegie at 16, with his only brother Thomas, age 10.

er mouth to feed. Mr. Carnegie had to sell all but one of his four looms and move the family into an even smaller cottage, where everyone shared one tiny upstairs room.

Andy's father seemed helpless in the face of disaster. He could not believe that the era of craftsmanship was over. A big steam-powered linen-weaving factory had recently opened close by, with 400 weavers glad to find jobs there. The machine had won; the weavers were through. The loom shops stood empty and shuttered along the streets of Dunfermline. Some craftsmen, applying too late to find jobs in the factory, were taking a day's work now and then in the hated coal mines, crawling on their bellies in the damp and dark.

News filtered in from Ireland and western Scotland that more than 300,000 people had starved to death from the potato blight. Would the typhus and cholera that followed in its wake soon reach eastern Scotland?

One day Will Carnegie came home from another fruit-less visit to the merchants who used to supply him work. This time he was told that he would never get another order to fill at his loom. It confirmed Margaret Carnegie's belief: The utopian dreams of her husband and brother would never be fulfilled. Society was not going to be improved by moral appeal, petition or demonstration. Look at reality! In this world the men who had the power and the wealth (are they not one and the same?) did not get them by being good-hearted and virtuous. No, they can credit their position as top dogs to their ruthless determination to have and to hold. Their values are drawn not from the teachings of Christ but from measuring the worth of everything in hard coin.

How to survive in such a world?

Andy's mother had an answer:

Let's move from this dying town. Let's do what some of family and friends have already done. Let's go to America!

Nearly 300,000 of their countrymen had already given up and fled to America. They did not go happily, but desperately. They were pushed by their utter failure to make it in their old home and pulled by the promise, however vague, of a better life in a new home.

Two of Mrs. Carnegie's sisters and their husbands had already emigrated to Pennsylvania. At first their letters were not encouraging, but recently their tone was brighter: "This country's far better for the working man than the old one, and there is room enough to spare. As for myself, I like it much better than at home, for in fact you seem to breathe a freer atmosphere here."

Andy's parents read those letters over and over again, debating whether to emigrate. Will, now 43, hopeless and worn out by worry, couldn't imagine emigrating; Margaret, 33, wanted nothing else, and she took control. She sold off household furnishings and Will's last loom, borrowed from a friend, and booked the cheapest passage on the sailing ship, *Wiscasset*.

The younger son, Tom, now five, was too young to understand what was happening. For Andy, 12, there was the sad sense of his father's failure and his mother's contempt for it. His mind was full of romantic notions of Scotland's past and hazy visions of a bright new life that he would help create in America.

On May 17, 1848, their ship sailed from Glasgow. It took seven weeks to reach New York City. From there they traveled by canal boat and steamboat to Allegheny, Pennsylvania (now part of Pittsburgh), where friends from home welcomed them. They lived rent-free for a time in a small dark frame house on a muddy alley. Owned by an aunt, the house had a weaver's shop in the back. Will Carnegie began weaving tablecloths and then going door-to-door in a futile effort to sell them. But his craft was just as dead in America as it was back home.

Pittsburgh, Pennsylvania, the industrial center where the Carnegie family settled

Again, Margaret came to the rescue. She knew how to make shoes, and from a cobbler nearby she got work binding shoes at home at night, after taking care of family and household chores during the day. Little Tom sat beside her, threading needles and waxing thread. As for Andy, he knew that his schooldays were over: "I fairly panted to get to work that I might help the family to a start in the new land."

With prices of necessities so low, the boy figured out that they would need to make $300 a year, or $25 monthly, to keep the family going without being dependent on others.

When no one wanted Will's tablecloths, he quit hand-loom weaving and took a job in a cotton mill owned by an old Scots friend. Andy too was hired, at $2 a week. He worked alone in the cellar, running the steam engine and firing the boiler. He recalled:

> *It was a hard life. In the winter, father and I had to rise and breakfast in the darkness, reach the factory before it was daylight, and with a short interval for lunch, work till after dark. The hours hung heavily upon me and in the work itself I took no pleasure . . . but it gave me the feeling that I was doing something for my world—our family.*

What else was open to the boy? He knew how to read and write and do figuring. He could recite many poems. The grim fact that the Carnegies were living under even worse conditions than at home didn't upset him. He had faith in America's political democracy, where the privileges of kings and lords didn't exist. Not to be born rich was no barrier to success. Any career was open to a boy with ambition, and his was boundless.

Where did such optimism, such self-confidence, come from? He seems to have been aggressive by nature, but that was softened by his great charm and his natural skill with words. Andy could talk almost anyone into anything. He had a strong tendency to romanticize the past, not only the historical past but his own personal past as well. Much later, in 1896, when America was suffering one of its worst depressions, he would say to young people:

> It is because I know how sweet and happy and pure the home of honest poverty is . . . that I sympathize with the rich man's boy . . . . It seems, nowadays, a matter of universal desire that poverty should be abolished. We should be quite willing to abolish luxury, but to abolish honest, industrious, self-denying poverty would be to destroy the soil upon which mankind produces the virtues which enable our race to reach a still higher civilization than it now possesses.

Reading this now may make you wince. Here is one of the world's wealthiest industrialists, employing thousands of poorly paid workers, preaching the virtues of poverty.

One day the mill owner asked Andy if he could write well enough to make out the company's bills. The boy took on the fresh task and soon was also handling the company's correspondence. Because this assignment did not take the whole day, the boss added another chore: dipping the newly made cotton spools in a vat of preservative oil. The stink of the oil was nauseating, and Andy would have quit if he had not remembered that his hero, William Wallace, never gave up in bad times.

So quit he could not, unless he could claim a better job. If he was to survive in a messy world, he must develop the skills to lift himself above the masses. He liked the clean work of keeping the company books. Yet the boss was still using the old single-entry system. Andy saw his opening. If he could master the superior double-entry system, he could ask for a full-time accountant's job.

That winter of 1848–49 he got three of his young friends to go into Pittsburgh with him a few nights a week to learn double-entry bookkeeping from an accountant. The logic of math and the pleasure of manipulating numbers delighted him. But before he could transform the mill's accounting, he got an unexpected break.

The telegraph had just come to Pittsburgh, and one evening over a game of checkers the manager of the local telegraph office told Andy's uncle that he needed another messenger boy. Andy got the job. This was 1850, and Andy was 14.

The sending of messages by the electric telegraph was the most startling technological transformation of that period. The scientific basis for it was developed in the mid-1830s at almost the same moment by several different researchers. Then, only a few years before Andy got his job, Samuel F. B. Morse figured out a way to signal over long distances by means of a simple electric circuit. What came out of Morse's device at the receiving end was a crude paper recording of dots and dashes—short and long bursts of current. A code was devised to express the letters of the alphabet and the numbers from zero to nine. It was a simple new language. Very soon operators like Andy would be able to "read" messages just from the clicking sound of the recording instrument. Several telegraph companies offered the service at first, but within ten years Western Union would bring the whole American telegraph system into one organization.

At first the telegraph was used by the railways, then, by the creation of underseas cables, it made rapid worldwide communication possible. Of course businesses were the heaviest users, but private citizens soon followed. The telegraph transformed the news, too. Scoops were no longer measured in days but in hours and minutes. It increased the demand for quick news and stimulated the enlargement of the newspapers. Messages that only yesterday would have taken weeks to communicate could now be sent and received in an instant.

Like any Horatio Alger hero, Andy set out to be the best in the telegraph office. Within a few weeks he had studiously memorized the names and locations of all the main streets in Pittsburgh, as well as of the chief firms. He lay awake nights trying to fix in his mind the names and faces of the members of Pittsburgh's growing business community to whom he delivered messages.

With his keen mind and observant eye Andy soon knew a great deal about Pittsburgh's business life. He learned who was making deals and at what profit or loss, who was seeking partners, who was fighting competitors, who was winning, and who was losing. Access to the telegraph messages became his school of business. It was training he would make good use of later on.

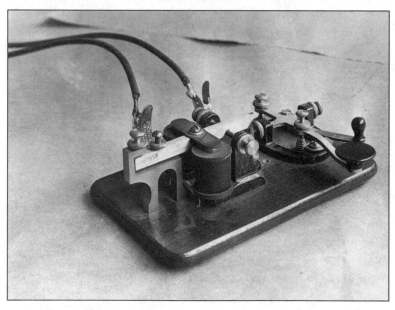

The early form of the telegraph instrument that young Carnegie mastered

And that was how, Carnegie later recalled:

I got my first real start in life. From the dark cellar running a steam engine at two dollars a week, begrimed with coal dirt, without a trace of the elevating influences of life, I was lifted into paradise, yes, heaven, as it seemed to me, with newspapers, pen, pencils, and sunshine about me. There was scarcely a minute in which I could not learn something or find out how much there was to learn and how little I knew. I felt that my foot was on the ladder and that I was bound to climb.

THREE

AMERICA WAS PROMISES

At the time Andy joined the telegraph company, the economy was in the midst of great change. The United States was moving its capital, manpower, and technology from the old agricultural system to the new industrial one. Wealthy merchants were shifting their surplus money from trade to manufacturing, with the banks quickly following.

In the changeover, Pittsburgh played a vital role. It was located on a main east-west route, at a meeting of great river systems. The waterways radiated from the city east toward iron mines and furnaces, south toward coal deposits, north toward iron and oil reserves. As these natural resources were discovered and developed, the rivers carried them to Pittsburgh. A major commercial center in the early 1800s, the city now added iron manufacturing to its strength.

By the time the Carnegies arrived, Pittsburgh's skies were already filled with smoke and the rivers covered with slime. Its houses were mostly of wood, easily destroyed by a devastating fire, such as the one of 1845. The population was about 40,000. Allegheny, where the Carnegies lived, was a separate community on the edge of the city with great open spaces.

Two telegraph lines had just entered Pittsburgh, one from the East Coast, the other from points west. There was as yet no direct rail connection with the East. It took three days to travel by canal and then by rail to reach Philadelphia. A steamboat linked Pittsburgh with Cincinnati in the west. A rolling mill had begun to produce iron, but steel manufacture was still a long way off.

Through Andy's job as messenger boy he met some of the leading business and political figures of Pittsburgh. He looked up to them as models of what he hoped to become. He was happy in his work, often winning compliments for his swift delivery. If a messenger had to travel beyond a fixed distance, he earned an extra ten cents—a sizable addition to the $2.50 a week the boys were paid. When trouble arose because such bonus messages were not evenly allocated, Andy proposed that they pool the dimes from all such messages and divide the cash equally at the end of each week. Because it was his idea, the boys appointed him treasurer—his first experience in "financial organization," he said.

Although he brought about peaceful agreement on the "dime messages," the other boys found Andy domineering. He arrogantly tried to regulate their morals, just as his mother had protected his. He himself would not use tobacco or liquor and showed contempt for those weak enough to indulge. He even reprimanded them for eating too much candy.

Working as a messenger boy wasn't easy. The hours were long, and every other evening the boys had to be on duty until the office closed. Often Andy didn't get home until 11 P.M. "It left little time for self-improvement," he said, and since his pay helped support the family, there was no money to buy books.

The office manager liked Andy's devotion to duty. He

put him in charge of assigning message delivery to the other boys. They resented his authority and the way he meddled in their affairs, but it didn't bother him. It was what his superiors thought of him that counted.

Singling Andy out, the manager gave him a modest raise in pay. His parents were overjoyed; a dollar or two more a month meant so much. Andy confided that he dreamed that some day they would own a big business together—the "Carnegie Brothers"—and become so rich they'd have their own carriages.

The messengers had to reach the office an hour before opening time in order to sweep floors and clean up any mess. The other boys hated the extra duty but Andy would finish his chores in a hurry and then go into the operating room to learn how to operate the telegraph instruments. He perfected his skill by sending and receiving practice messages with boys in other telegraph offices along the line.

His burning need to make good brought results. The manager let him relieve other operators during break time. And soon he was promoted from messenger to operator. Now he was earning the grand sum of $20 a month.

Mrs. Carnegie, continuing her shoe binding, was also helping out in her sister's grocery store. Tom was in school, hoping to soon find work in the telegraph office. But Will Carnegie, showing little of his son's energy and adaptability, was unable to pull himself out of his deep depression. It made things only worse when it became clear that his boy was now the chief support of the family. Even politics failed to interest the old radical.

But Andy was not indifferent to what was going on. This was the decade—the 1850s—that saw a long and stormy debate in Congress over the extension of slavery in the territories. The United States had grown enormously through its recent aggression against Mexico. Many justified that war in the belief that it was America's destiny to rule the whole continent—peacefully, if possible, by force if necessary. Clinging to the radical views of his family, Andy was still a pacifist. Yet he tended to pocket his principles when he saw personal advantage in doing so. For him America was promises, nothing but glorious promises; he shut his eyes to reality.

"I take great interest in politics here," he wrote his Uncle Lauder, "and when I am a man I would like to dabble a little in them. . . . Slavery I hope will soon be abolished."

His last step in Americanizing himself was to wipe out his Scottish accent. He never lost his enthusiasm for Wallace, Bruce, and Burns or his pride in his Scottish origin. But like many immigrants, he wanted badly to be considered as American as anyone else. But with Andy there was one difference. He would never be content to be simply like "anyone." He must be "someone"—different, superior.

Rapid as his rise was from messenger to operator, Andy was eager to do better. He heard of an operator who could take a message by "reading" the sound of the key rather than its printout. Soon he too was taking messages by ear. So rare was this dazzling skill that businessmen hearing of it would drop by the office just to see the boy wonder perform. Impressed by this achievement, they began to ask for his personal services. Up and up he went: more responsibility, more pay, and soon enough savings for the Carnegies to put a down payment on their own house.

One evening, taking a dispatch to a passenger boat heading downriver, Andy ran into his father. Will Carnegie was going to Cincinnati hoping to sell a few of the tablecloths he was still turning out on his loom. The weather was raw, cold, and rainy, yet Will, unable to pay cabin passage, was spending the night on the open deck, like a homeless peddler.

The contrast between the two, father on the open deck,

son in a stateroom, was painfully clear to both. The boy, only sixteen, was already so businesslike, so self-confident, while the father was sunk in utter defeat. Trying to comfort Will, Andy said, "Father, it will not be long before mother and you shall ride in your carriage." In answer, Will took his son's hand and, in a faltering voice, said, "Andy, I am proud of you."

Long after this encounter Carnegie recorded it in his autobiography. The passage of time had given him no deeper insight into how insensitive he had been to his father's feelings. He never realized how he was rubbing it in to a father who had failed. For a man who would never know failure himself, there was little sympathy or under-standing for those who did fail.

Busy as he was at work, Andy found time for tasting life's pleasures. He got up early on Sunday mornings dur-ing winter to skate on the river before going to church. He talked some young friends into forming a debating club. They met in a cobbler's shop to debate current issues, with Andy notorious for speaking 90 minutes—without pause—in defense of his side.

What he learned from this early training helped him when he faced many audiences in years to come.

He had never been in a theater until one evening the local manager of the playhouse let him slip upstairs to the second balcony to see a performance of *Macbeth*. It was his introduction to Shakespeare, and he was as thrilled by the music of the words as he had been by the poetry of Burns. He determined to read all Shakespeare's plays and to mem-orize the best parts.

But getting his hands on books was no easy task. There was no public library. He borrowed a book or two from friends. But one day he read in the newspaper that Colonel James Anderson of Allegheny was opening his personal library of four hundred volumes on Saturday afternoons to young workers who wished to borrow a book for a week. Andy took out books on history, on the sciences, on philosophy. "The intellectual wealth of this world was opened to me," he said. "I reveled week after week in books."

Delighted with the results of his experiment, Anderson expanded and added several hundred volumes to his collection and placed it in a building of its own. "The Mechanics and Apprentices Library" became Allegheny's first public library. But Anderson had called for an annual fee of two dollars for all users except apprentices. Andy objected strenuously to that limitation (he was no apprentice!) and wrote a letter of complaint to Pittsburgh's leading newspaper, signing it "A Working Boy." The paper published it. This led to his meeting Colonel Anderson. Anderson admitted Andy was right and agreed to change the terms of his gift so all working boys, whether apprentices or not, could borrow books free.

Then and there, Andy resolved that "if ever wealth came to me, it should be used to establish free libraries, that other poor boys might receive opportunities similar to those for which we were indebted to that noble man."

It was a triumph for Andy. Not only had he won his point, but he had the thrill of seeing his words in print. Maybe he could become a journalist? Whatever was around the corner, he was ready for it.

MONEY MAKES MONEY

It happened quicker than anyone expected. In December 1852 the Pennsylvania Railroad Company opened a continuous single-track rail line between Pittsburgh and Philadelphia. Now Pittsburgh was no longer dependent on canals, lakes, and rivers to move people and freight between east and west.

It was a great break for the telegraph office. An important customer was now even bigger. Tom Scott, only 30, was the new superintendent of the Pennsylvania's western division. He came into the wire office often and was impressed by Andy's cheerful manner and his ability to get the job done quickly and well. Soon he was giving all his wire traffic to Andy, calling him "my white-haired Scotch devil."

In just a few weeks Scott decided he needed his own telegraph operator with a wire running directly from his office to points east on the railroad. He offered young Carnegie the job. Andy stalled a bit, angling to get the biggest possible raise. He settled for $35 a month and began his new job on February 1, 1853. No longer did he have to work nights till 11; now he was done at 6. Best of all, he was sure that at the Pennsylvania he was bound to rise much faster.

Serving Scott as private secretary as well as personal telegraph operator, Andy acquired a rich knowledge of railroading. Now after a seasoning in communications, he was in on the ground floor of another great enterprise—transportation. Both were powerful forces in America's march toward industrialization. The first railroad tracks

Thomas A. Scott, the rising star of the Pennsylvania Railroad. He hired 17-year-old Carnegie as his personal telegrapher and promoted him to be his secretary. At 24, Carnegie was made superintendent of the railroad's western division.

had been laid in Maryland in 1828. By 1840 America had 3,000 miles of track, and in the 1850s, another 20,000 miles would be built, with rail links stretching as far west as the Mississippi River.

The connection between telegraph and railroad became very close. Each was of great value to the other. Because the telegraph lines followed the rail lines, they could help each other. When railroads were built, trees were cleared back from the right of way, leaving ample room for telegraph poles to be erected. And the train crews could always observe where a break in the telegraph line had occurred so it could be quickly repaired.

The value of the telegraph to the railroad was perhaps even greater, especially when the trains ran on single-track systems. Telegraph operators in the train stations could wire up or down the line to let station agents know whether trains were delayed or whether they needed to be held up or moved ahead. Eventually a prerequisite for the station agent's job became knowledge of telegraph operation.

Andy soaked up every scrap of knowledge he could on the new job. Every message, every bill of lading, taught him something about sender and receiver, and he sized up each customer who came by the office for his management skill. He came to know almost as much about Pittsburgh's business world as did its leaders.

Intelligent, efficient, enterprising: he proved his qualities every day on the job. But he was not immune from making mistakes. One day he was sent to Altoona to pick up the monthly payroll for the employees in the Pittsburgh area. He wrapped the payroll and the checks in a bundle and fastened them inside his jacket. Instead of sitting in a passenger car, he got permission to ride up front in the cab of the locomotive so he could watch how the engineer and the fireman did their jobs.

As the train approached a station en route Andy casually reached inside his jacket to make sure the bundle was safe. He was horrified to find it missing. The loss would surely mean the end of his job with the Pennsylvania. He begged the engineer to back up the train slowly so he could examine every inch of the ground for a trace of the missing payroll. The engineer obliged. As the train backed across a bridge Andy spotted the bundle lying below on the bank, only a foot away from the water. He leaped off the locomotive, ran down the embankment, and snatched up the bundle.

That one piece of carelessness could have cost him dearly. He would have lost the confidence of everyone who had helped him. In his autobiography Carnegie said the incident taught him never to be too hard on any employee even if he does commit a dreadful mistake or two. But that was hardly the truth. When he became the big boss of his own enterprises he would not tolerate error. In fact, within a few weeks of the near loss of the payroll, when Scott was away and left him in charge of the office, Carnegie abruptly fired a man for negligence.

Scott was startled by Andy's tough drill-sergeant behavior. This was no ordinary clerk doing his job routinely. Scott was in for another surprise when an unsigned letter defending the Pennsylvania against criticism by some Pittsburgh businessmen appeared in a Pittsburgh newspaper. Who had written it? Andy confessed that he was the author, surprising Scott by his literary talent. This was the second time Carnegie found how useful a weapon the pen could be.

A much greater proof of how capable the young Carnegie was came when Scott was away, and Andy, alone in the office, got a message that a serious accident had occurred on the railroad. All traffic east and west would be held up indefinitely unless a way out of the terrible snarl could be figured out. Carnegie made quick decisions, wired his orders to all concerned, and restored order to the Pennsylvania.

When Scott came in, Andy told him what he had done,

fearing his presumptuous act might get him fired. But Scott was pleased by this fresh proof of Carnegie's talents and bragged to others of what a find this young man was. The president of the railroad, J. Edgar Thomson, heard of Andy's exploits, and on his next trip to Pittsburgh came into the telegraph room to look the young man over. "So you're Scott's Andy!" he said admiringly.

Although Andy was earning a good salary, his family had to keep pinching pennies to complete payment on the home under the two-year contract. Will Carnegie was unable to put anything into the pot. He still went to his loom daily, but his tablecloths and piece goods ended in closet storage. No one wanted to buy. In the spring of 1855 he gave up on work, and on life. He lay in bed for months, silent and withdrawn. The doctor was unable to find any-thing he could diagnose as an illness. And then, in October, Will died. He was 51.

The family grieved, but Will's death did not affect their economic well-being. Andy was still the chief wage earner, Margaret continued her nighttime cobbling and her day-time clerking, and Tom, now 12, was entering high school.

Andy and his mother remained as close as ever. She would offer her guidance and support until the day she died, whether he asked for it or not. Although he became a powerful leader, he would never marry while his mother still lived.

It was not that he didn't like girls. His social life was full and happy. Full-grown now, he was a small man, only five feet three inches tall at a time when the average man's height was five feet seven inches. His liveliness and quick wit made him popular. He enjoyed the company of both men and women as they went skating on the river, read plays together, or sang at weekly choir sessions. The debating club continued to meet regularly, with Andy standing out for his radical views on slavery, politics, and religion. When the Kansas-Nebraska Act of 1854 opened the territories to slavery, he felt the American people had been betrayed. He wrote an antislavery editorial, sent it to Horace Greeley's *New York Tribune,* and saw it published. Although still too young to vote, he endorsed the new Republican Party—which had been formed in opposition to the expansion of slavery—when it held its first national meeting in Pittsburgh in 1856.

Regarding religion, Andy was a skeptic like his mother. He could support no church. He broke free from dogma, coming to believe that "A forgiving God was the noblest work of man."

As for American democracy, Andy could see no flaws in it. Yes, slavery was evil, but that would soon be cured. There might be other things wrong, he admitted, but these would improve or disappear because the system was self-correcting. He liked to compare America with other countries—Britain or Canada, for example—asking what did they have to show that could match the achievements of the United States?

It was a handy faith that excused all sorts of abuses and rejected any attempt by government or labor to bring about reforms. As the press in the post–Civil War years began to expose widespread political corruption and economic abuse, Carnegie did not change his views. He himself would be guilty of some of that corruption and abuse.

One day early in 1856 Tom Scott told Andy that ten shares of a very sound stock, the Adams Express Company, were available. Would he like to make a good investment? He would—but with what? The price was $610, and he didn't have even a tiny fraction of that saved up. So Scott lent him the money. To pay it back by the set date, Carnegie had to borrow the money from someone else. And to pay *that* back, his mother had to raise the money by taking out a mortgage on their house.

It was a complex financial operation, Andy's first venture into the world of capitalism. Young as he was, with no experience in finance, he saw how to manipulate money to his advantage. The payoff began to come in when his first Adams dividend check arrived—ten dollars. "I shall remember that check as long as I live," he said. "It gave me the first penny of revenue from capital—something that I had not worked for with the sweat of my brow." He had discovered "the goose that lays the golden eggs."

His friends were astounded. None of them had imagined how money could make money, with no labor demanded of the investor.

That fall, Scott was promoted to general superintendent of the Pennsylvania; it meant moving to Altoona. He took Carnegie with him as his secretary, raising his pay to $50 a month.

They met trouble as soon as they arrived in Altoona. There had been short strikes on the line by the freight-car workers in recent months, and now the maintenance crews too threatened to go out on the picket line. One evening a man stopped Andy on his way home from work and said he wanted to return the favor Andy had done when he had helped him get a job as a blacksmith on the railroad. Then the man handed Carnegie a list of all the men who had just signed a pledge to go on strike. The next morning Scott posted a notice in all the Pennsy shops with the names of the men who had signed the pledge. Come in for your final paycheck, it said. You're all fired.

What a long way this was from Carnegie's childhood in radical Dunfermline where informers were the most hated people in the community. To be a company or government spy was an abomination. Yet Carnegie blotted out that memory. Retelling the incident he said nothing about the cause of the strikes. He drew the conclusion that if you "do a kindness to a poor workingman, he may be able to repay the favor." In this case, that meant informing on his fellow workers.

Carnegie always liked to romanticize his experiences, giving them a golden, sentimental glow that made him look virtuous or brilliant and deserving of all the wonderful things fortune brought him. Take another investment he made. No sooner had railroads begun to spread through the country than people began to see the need to make night travel more comfortable by providing berths for sleeping. Theodore T. Woodruff, an inventor and master car-builder, had patented a sleeping care in 1856 and now was seeking capital to expand production of them.

Years later Carnegie took all the credit for Woodruff's success. He wrote that one day, riding on a train, he was approached by another passenger who drew out of a green bag a small model for a sleeper berth for use on railroads. Carnegie wrote that he immediately saw what a marvelous invention this was and promised Woodruff (for that's who the stranger was) that he would tell Tom Scott about it. The Pennsylvania tried it out, and "a triumphant success was scored."

When this account appeared in a book of Carnegie's, Woodruff was furious. He wrote to his alleged discoverer, informing him that his sleeping cars were being used on several railroads before he had even asked the Pennsylvania to use them. Woodruff reminded Carnegie that he initiated the order, going first to the line's president, Mr. Thomson, who had then referred him to Scott. You, Carnegie, he added, had nothing to do with it.

When Scott negotiated a contract with Woodruff he asked that an interest in it be reserved for a young man in his office. This was typical of many favors Scott did for "my Andy." Carnegie put up $217.50 for his share, to be paid out of dividends. Thus without spending a dollar of his own, within two years the investment was bringing him an annual income of $5,000, more than three times his yearly salary on the railroad.

As soon as possible, Andy brought his mother and brother to live with him in Altoona. He insisted they hire a servant (successful men all had them) and then another and another. Carnegie lamented that "being served by others is a poor substitute for a mother's labor of love." One wonders if his long overworked mother would have preferred to slave in the kitchen all her days.

In 1859, after three years in Altoona, Scott was promoted to vice president of the railroad, with headquarters in Philadelphia.

What will happen to me? Andy wondered. Scott had a ready reply: "Do you think you could manage the Pittsburgh Division?"

This was an easy question for the brash young man to answer. Carnegie recalled, "I was at an age when I thought I could manage anything. I knew nothing that I would not attempt." Well, what about your salary? Scott asked. "Salary?" said Carnegie, "What do I care about salary? I want the position." The important thing was for him to have the department for himself, to be able to sign AC to all orders, not Scott's initials. Scott insisted he take the same salary Scott had when he ran the division: $1,200 a year.

Word went out to all employees on the western division that on December 1, 1859, they would be under the charge of Andrew Carnegie, the new superintendent.

A DARING INNOVATOR

In December the Carnegies were back in Pittsburgh, happy to be close to their old friends. But they did not live in the same neighborhood. They rented a bigger house, in the center of the city. In Altoona they had enjoyed the fresh mountain air and a flower garden. Pittsburgh seemed worse than ever now. They sky was dark with smoke, soot blackened every surface, green life perished where the sun never came through. Soon the family moved out to Homewood, a suburb 15 miles northeast of the city. They bought a two-story frame house, set amid spruce trees, green lawns, and flower beds.

Most of their neighbors were rich. They invited the young superintendent into their homes, where he heard talk of subjects he had never known before. Carnegie later recalled, "I made it a rule to learn something about them at once. I began to pay strict attention to my language, and to the English classics. . . . I began also to notice how much better it was to be gentle in tone and matter, polite and courteous to all – in short, better behaved." It was now that he "first realized the immeasurable gulf that separates the highly educated from people like myself."

Carnegie came to his new responsibility with a wealth of experience. He was lucky to be close to the seat of power in a business that created the pattern for the giant enterprises that would soon dominate the American economy. The railroads in the 1850s were by far the largest industrial units. Their size, their spread over huge territories, and their complexity of structure and operations were the proving ground for a managerial revolution that in a very brief period brought more change in how business decisions were made and operating methods devised than had occurred in centuries. Carnegie saw the way railroads were constructed and financed and the way they were run. He saw how tracks and rolling stock were manufactured, how services were priced, how charges were collected, how profits were calculated.

He learned that such a complex business left no room for casual operations. With the telegraph, quick and complete information controlled the movement of trains. Safety on the line required intelligent and highly disciplined workers. The complexity of equipment demanded that many specialized skills be coordinated. Managers had to deal with boilermakers, pipefitters, carpenters, sheet metal workers, mechanics, track inspectors, and telegraph and signal maintenance men. Although they were all experts, if they were not carefully organized they could get in each other's way and jam up the works.

The number-one requirement was discipline. The Pennsylvania put out a book of rules, rules that had to be enforced at every level of management. Each worker's responsibility and authority was spelled out. And if they failed to perform according to the standard, they were suspended, demoted, or dismissed.

It was an unbelievably rapid change from the old casual preindustrial society. The largest nonrailroad employer in the 1850s was a textile mill in New England. It had 800 workers; but the Pennsylvania had 4,000.

Carnegie learned how precise he had to be. Prices charged on the line for services were based on actual costs, not guesswork or the vague operations of market forces. The goal was to provide "the minimum amount of service consistent with the largest net revenue." He grasped the formula for profitable operation of a large enterprise: learn the costs and reduce them as much as possible, and then lower prices to attract a greater volume of business.

By the time Carnegie was made chief of the western division, the Pennsylvania was approaching its peak: it would soon be the largest private business firm in the world in revenues, employees, and value of physical assets.

Carnegie shone as chief of the western division. He understood what had brought Pennsylvania to the top of its field. Tested by almost daily challenges, he proved himself a daring innovator. When wrecks occurred he cleared the line by burning cars or by laying track around them. He decided to keep telegraph offices open around the clock so trains could run on a 24-hour schedule. He had a special telegraph line put in his home so he'd never be out of touch with the Pittsburgh office. He proposed making improvements in services and in cost-cutting, backed by hard statistical facts that headquarters accepted. To eliminate a crew change between Altoona and Pittsburgh he made train crews work 13-hour instead of 10-hour shifts. He cut commuting fares to meet competition and keep his trains full. Traffic multiplied on the line as it expanded road mileage, and profits stayed high.

Carnegie knew that he himself was being tested. President Thomson surely had doubts about so young a man running his western division. Sweating to make good, Carnegie pushed himself as hard as he did his employees. That first winter on the job was a very harsh one, but he went out in all kinds of weather. Once, when a freight train was derailed, he bundled himself into the same rough clothing the crews wore and rushed to the scene to supervise clearing the line. When he only got in the way, a big Irishman lifted him up off the ground and set him to one side. "Get out of the way, you brat of a boy," he growled. "You're eternally in the way of men who are trying to do their job."

Carnegie loved to tell the story on himself in later years, but at the time he must have been furious. Soon after, he began to grow a thin fringe of beard which framed his boyish face, but it didn't really make him look any older.

Some employers might fear the charge of nepotism if they hired family or friends but not Carnegie. He made his brother Tom, now 16, his personal secretary and appointed a cousin, Maria Hogan, as a telegraph operator. She was the first woman operator in the country, and she would train other women for the same work.

In 1861 the Civil War broke out. As Carnegie recalled it, "I was at once summoned to Washington by Mr. Scott, who had been appointed Assistant Secretary of War in charge of the Transportation Department. I was to act as his assistant in charge of the military railroads and telegraphs of the Government and to organize a force of railroad men."

This is how Carnegie in his autobiography introduced the Civil War and his role in it. What he skips is telling of the decision every young Northerner faced when President Lincoln called for 75,000 volunteers for three month's service. Few saw that this would be no 90-day fight but the bloodiest war of the 19th century.

The war began April 12, 1861, when Southern troops fired on the Union's Fort Sumter in Charleston Harbor. A great surge of patriotic feeling swept cities and farms of the North at the news that the flag and American troops had been fired upon by slaveholders. Young workers and farmers flocked to the colors at Lincoln's call.

But not every man of military age , however, respond-

Early in the Civil War, Carnegie helped organize rail and telegraph connections for the Union Army. Here, soldiers set up a telegraph wire during combat.

ed to the call-to-arms. There were a number of practical, hardheaded young men who did not go to war: J. P. Morgan, John D. Rockefeller, Philip Armour, James Hill, Jay Gould, Jim Fisk, Andrew Carnegie—all in their twenties. While others died, they stayed safe, laying the basis of great American fortunes. "Only greenhorns enlist," wrote Judge Thomas Mellon, one of Carnegie's most admired Pittsburghers, to his son. "Here there is no credit to going. All stay if they can and go if they must."

Whether Carnegie felt the impulse to volunteer he never says. He answered Scott's summons to serve as a civilian and moved toward Washington with a small corps of handpicked railroad men. He did an excellent job, repairing tracks torn up by Confederate sympathizers, preventing the capital from being cut off from the North, and bringing troops to wherever they were needed. It was the first war in which the control of railroad lines was crucial. Under Scott's supervision, Carnegie organized the railroad and telegraph communications south into Virginia and put together the first U.S. Military Telegraphers Corps.

When the Union forces retreated from their defeat at Bull Run, Carnegie and his crews kept the trains filled with wounded running back to the hospitals in Washington.

In those early months of the war he did the hardest physical labor of his life. As he wrote to a friend:

> I am delighted with my occupation here, hard work—but how gratifying to lie down at night and think By George you are of some use in sustaining a great cause and making the path clearer for those who come hereafter as well as maintaining the position that humanity has, after all laborious efforts, succeeded in reaching.

He suffered minor harm twice: a gash across his cheek and forehead while helping to repair a broken telegraph line and sunstroke when rebuilding a railroad bridge.

Compensating for such injury was the chance to see much of Lincoln. The president often came to Carnegie's telegraph office in the War Department and anxiously watched the dispatches come in from the battlefronts. Carnegie remembered the president as

> one of the most homely men I ever saw when his features were in repose. When excited or telling a story, intellect shone through his eyes and illuminated his face to a degree which I have seldom or never seen in any other. . . . I never met a great man who so thoroughly made himself one with all men as Mr. Lincoln.

By early autumn of 1861 Carnegie was gone from Washington, his brief wartime duty ended. After his sunstroke he feared that in his weakened condition he might catch typhoid, which was sweeping through the camps near the capital. He argued with Scott that he would be of more service to the cause at his old job as head of the Pennsylvania's western division. Scott agreed, reluctantly.

The mark made by the Civil War on the rest of the country was enormous. It freed four million African-Americans from slavery. It brought about the deaths of 600,000 Union and Confederate soldiers. No community in the country escaped its physical and personal effects.

When Carnegie returned to Pittsburgh he found the city pushing harder than ever to seize the opportunity offered by the war to make big profits. New machines and new processes were being developed, and as the level of technology advanced, the makers and doers were fired by the belief that everything was up for grabs. As others dug the coal and gold, welded the engines, laid the tracks, strung the wires, the young men of '61 instead used their nimble brains and their tireless energy to make themselves ever richer.

Whether it meant to or not, Lincoln's Republican Party unleashed the full force of the industrial revolution. The Homestead Act began to parcel out the public domain. As the historian Matthew Josephson wrote, "In a hurried partition, for nominal sums or by cession, this benevolent government handed over to its friends or the astute first comers . . . all those treasures of coal and oil, of copper and gold and iron, the land grants, the terminal sites, the perpetual rights of way—an act of largesse which is still one of the wonders of history."

In addition, money subsidies in the hundreds of millions were given to the railroads. A tariff law provided a sheltering wall of subsidies. To aid the heavy industries in need of manpower an immigration law invited the free importation of cheap contract labor. And last but not least, a "due process clause" was inserted into the Fourteenth

Carnegie (at left) with two of his partners, George Lauder and Tom Miller, in their early years as entrepreneurs

Amendment, which the Supreme Court transformed from its original intended defense of the civil rights of African Americans into the bulwark of property rights.

The bright young men of these years saw their chance, and each in his own way, as Josephson put it, "rushed to seize the resources, the key positions of the industrial society being hastily assembled. They would find themselves, incredibly enough, commanders of strongholds, lords of 'empires' in iron, beef, railroads or oil, to be held naturally for private gain, and once held, defended by them to the last breath of financial life against all comers."

Andrew Carnegie was one of those bright young men.

CUT COSTS!
CUT COSTS!

Back in his superintendent's office of the western division, Carnegie applied his old rule: expand, reduce costs, increase company profits. Without neglecting the Pennsylvania, however, he began to pay more attention to personal investments. One of his first was in an oil field in Pennsylvania. He used his dividends from the Woodruff Sleeping Car Company to buy about one thousand shares. It turned out to be one of the most profitable investments he would ever make. Some of his money went into still other enterprises—a telegraph company, an iron forge, a bank. At the end of 1863 his annual income was close to $50,000. Looking at it in terms of interest upon principal, it was almost a millionaire's income. "I'm rich! I'm rich!" he exclaimed with delight when a friend asked him how he was doing.

Through his railroad experience Carnegie saw the possibilities in manufacturing heavy equipment needed by the ever-expanding lines. He realized that the wooden bridges then used on the railways would not do for the future. Iron bridges must soon replace them. So he organized a company in Pittsburgh to make them. He borrowed the start-up money from a bank. His Keystone Bridge Company was the first successful manufacturer of iron railway bridges.

Carnegie loved bridges; he saw these great engineering feats as testimonials to the national spirit. His company not only built them, but he also sold bonds to help finance them, as well as other enterprises, drawing still more profit from commissions on these financial transactions. When Carnegie saw that not enough rails were being made to replace the dangerously old ones, he organized a railmaking company in Pittsburgh.

His yearly salary at the Pennsylvania railroad, $2,400, was a measly sum compared with his other income. Why should he continue to put out so much time and energy for so small a reward? He told himself he had to do it because it was his contribution to the war effort. But would the fighting never end? It went on and on, year after year. But deep in his increasingly complex business affairs, the bloody battlegrounds seemed so remote.

Then in the summer of 1864, came a terrible surprise. Carnegie was drafted for military service. He had never thought it possible, although he was 28 and unmarried. Had he not already given many months to the war effort as a civilian? And even suffered injury? Was he not worth more to the cause in his job on the Pennsylvania?

The draft law of 1863 said a man could avoid military service if he paid the government $300 or induced a substitute to go in his place. Three hundred dollars was a cheap price to pay for life, especially when life at home was proving more profitable every day of the war. Mr. Rockefeller had gladly paid the price, and so had Mr. Morgan and many other prosperous gentlemen.

Carnegie decided he too would get out of serving. Could he not do much more for the war by running the Pennsylvania than by slogging through mud in the field? The payment of $300 seemed too crass to him; he would find a substitute instead. Through a draft agent he got a young immigrant from Ireland to go in his place. It cost him $850, but it got Carnegie out of the draft.

Carnegie's interest in the Keystone company led him to conclude that wrought iron would inevitably replace cast iron. With his brother, Tom, and three friends he bought into a small company founded by Andrew Kloman that produced the best railroad axles on the market. Carnegie knew it because his division was Kloman's best customer. Kloman, a German immigrant, was a superb mechanic whose many inventions constantly improved production.

As other companies turned themselves into corporations they distributed their profits in dividends to their stockholders instead of plowing them back into improving production and lowering costs. And by refusing to raise the salaries of their best men, they often lost them to competitors who were not so tightfisted.

Carnegie operated differently. He kept any company in which he had a controlling interest a simple partnership. He held his most talented staff close, but not by giving them pay hikes or dividends. He believed that if he paid his executives tubs of money they didn't work as hard or apply themselves as much. Carnegie was willing to pay high, but only after the work was done. His method was to reward his top people with a small percentage of the ownership. They knew that if they stayed with him, some day they would accumulate a fortune. It spurred them to produce their best work at the lowest possible cost.

The secret—if it can be called that—of Carnegie's success in business was his stress on the cost of production, not the profits of production. Reinvest the profits in the company. Search out the greatest talents, the best scientific minds, and put them to work constantly improving the product. This is no secret, really, but hardly any other business leaders of his time followed in his path.

It sounds like the man never rested or had any fun, but this is not true. In the spring of 1862, as he was recovering from a serious illness, his doctor advised him to take a long holiday. The railroad granted him a three-month leave. It would be his first vacation in the 14 years since he had arrived in America. He had no problem deciding what to do. With his mother he sailed for Scotland to once again see his uncles, aunts, and cousins, his old schoolmates and childhood friends. Of course he traveled first class this time, and the crossing in the best steamer took two weeks, not seven.

The whole family turned out to greet them when they reached Dunfermline. But Carnegie was disappointed in what he found. Everything looked the same in Dunfermline, nothing had changed. And that was the trouble. Time had stood still for the home folks, while in America, his adopted home, everything was in constant flux. As he saw it, the changes were always for the better.

Most shocking to Carnegie upon his return to Scotland was the revelation that his old radical associates were pro-Confederate. They took the side of the Southern aristocracy in the Civil War, not the side of the progressive, antislavery forces of the Union democracy. Their press ridiculed Lincoln and advocated British intervention on the side of the slaveholders.

Carnegie's mother, Margaret Morrison Carnegie

Carnegie had arrived in Scotland during its worst economic depression in decades. And many of the unemployed cotton textile workers blamed the Union blockade for their misery. Only Andy's Uncle Lauder took the Union side during the noisy arguments.

Making the trip even worse, Carnegie came down with pneumonia while hiking through the cold and wet countryside. For six weeks he lay abed while the ancient treatment—bleeding—only weakened him more. As soon as he mustered enough strength, his mother took him back to America.

It had been a poor first vacation, but many others far more joyous would follow.

During Carnegie's early years in iron manufacturing he was greatly surprised to find that the cost of each process was unknown. Only at the end of the year when manufacturers balanced their books did they know whether they had a loss or a profit. To him this was an intolerable situation. He began making changes in his own businesses, introducing a system of accounting so that he knew not only what every department in the company was doing but what each man working at each job was doing. Thus he was able to compare one person's productivity with another's. The responsibility for what was being done with money or materials was brought home to every man. It enabled management to quickly detect what was being wasted and what was being best used.

Costs, costs, costs: He was always asking, what are they? And he was always demanding that they be reduced. That, "to a large measure," said his biographer Joseph Wall, was "the secret of his success."

It took years to develop and install his principles of management. It produced clear lines of authority, with specific rules and regulations to control all aspects of operations. But even though orders came from above, local foremen and supervisors had much to say about hiring, firing, work assignments, compensation rates, fringe benefits, discipline, and retirement. Many large-scale enterprises functioned this way. Often it meant favoring friends or relatives.

Early in 1865 Carnegie felt it was time to leave the Pennsylvania and give all his energy to his own affairs: "I was determined to make a fortune, and I saw no means of doing this honestly at any salary the railroad could afford to give." He resigned at the end of March and never again worked for a salary. Scarcely a week later, the South surrendered. The Civil War was over.

With the coming of peace, planning for the long-awaited transcontinental railroad rushed ahead. Carnegie saw in the great railroad enterprise the chance to promote his sleeping car, telegraph, and bridge-building companies, for all of them would be needed now.

Free from his job, Carnegie expanded the Keystone company, gaining contracts to build most of the major new bridges during the postwar boom, bridges that spanned the Missouri, Mississippi, the Ohio, and the climactic achievement—the Brooklyn Bridge.

Soaring over the East River linking Manhattan with Brooklyn, it became the most famous bridge in the world. An engineering miracle, the press called it. It was designed by John Roebling in 1867. The buttressed towers of the bridge, rising 272 feet above the water, are made entirely of granite. The platform, 86 feet wide, is hung on 2-inch diameter steel suspenders strung from two pairs of cables, 16 inches in diameter. Each cable is composed of 5,296 galvanized steel wires. The total length of wire used is 14,357 miles, a distance of more than half the circumference of the earth.

Putting in the lowest bid, Carnegie won the contract for the superstructure of the bridge. He had to adapt his steel production to meet the special requirements of the bridge's designers. He went to great expense and trouble, anticipating the great publicity that would come from the enter-

The Brooklyn Bridge, one of the many bridges that Carnegie's company built

prise. It led to other contracts for bridges in Mexico and South America and for the steel in the elevated railways of New York City.

By this time Carnegie was inspired by more than the profit motive. He felt great pride in knowing that his name, Andrew Carnegie, would be stamped on projects the world would long admire. They provided necessary services—carrying foot, wagon, rail, and eventually motor vehicle traffic across the continent—while also representing mighty monuments to technical genius and artistic design. Not the least pleasure for Carnegie were the profits of the bridge contracts themselves—the shares of the railroads using the bridges and the commissions for selling the bonds of the companies involved. Wherever the potential for profit pointed, he was there to realize it.

Neither an engineer nor a mechanic, Carnegie knew nothing about bridge construction. But he was a genius at finding the right talents, giving them a share in the business, and judging them by the results. If they did well they got a bigger share of the business; if they failed they were fired.

In the fall of 1867, Carnegie and his mother left Pittsburgh. His brother, Tom, had just married, and Carnegie gave the new couple his house in Homewood. As his businesses diversified, he often had to go to New York to take care of them. He felt it made more sense to establish a home and office at the center of the financial world. At first they moved into the sumptuous St. Nicholas Hotel, on Broadway in lower Manhattan. Later, he moved uptown to the new Windsor Hotel.

In New York he joined the Nineteenth Century Club, which met monthly to discuss political and cultural issues. There he got to know many celebrated people who, as he said, were great "educative" influences upon him. Now and then he himself spoke to the club, "excellent training" for his mind, for he had to study hard for each of his talks.

That same year he spent several months touring Europe with two friends. Up to this time he had known little of the fine arts, and now he made a determined effort to acquire knowledge of music, painting, and sculpture. But he would never neglect his commercial interests. In England he learned of a new coal-washing process and on his return home advanced the capital to build the first such machinery in America.

That year also saw Carnegie cement an alliance with George Pullman. Pullman had taken a trip in one of the Woodruff sleeping cars and decided to develop his own luxurious model. By 1867 he had 48 of them in use and wanted more.

In 1867 Carnegie and his mother moved from Pittsburgh to New York's newest and most luxurious hotel, the St. Nicholas.

A great coup would be to win the contract for sleeping cars from the Union Pacific Railroad, which was planning a transcontinental line. The Woodruff company, in which Carnegie had a strong share, was competing for the same contract. Carnegie proposed that Woodruff and Pullman would both do better if they formed a united company. "What would we call it?" Pullman asked. Appealing to the man's vanity, Carnegie answered, "The Pullman Palace Car Company!" It was a masterstroke. They made a deal and won the contract.

In his autobiography Carnegie claims that "A great business is seldom if ever built up, except on lines of the

One of the elegant new Pullman cars in which Carnegie invested

strictest integrity. A reputation for sharp dealing is fatal to great affairs. Not the letter of the law, but the spirit must be the rule. The standard of commercial morality is now very high. Always give the other party the benefit of the doubt."

Then, he warns, "This, of course, does not apply to the speculative class. An entirely different atmosphere pervades that world. Men are only gamblers there. Stock gambling and honorable business are incompatible."

But did he always operate "on lines of strictest integrity? And should a man give all his powers to the making of money? Was there something else worth living for?"

SEVEN

A MEMO
TO HIMSELF

As he turned 33 toward the end of 1868, Carnegie's conscience began to trouble him. Why should it? Wasn't he a great success? As if to prove it, he took a sheet of paper from his desk in his handsome hotel suite and added up his profits for the year. But his self-satisfaction quickly turned to self-criticism as he went on with this memo to himself:

Thirty-three and an income of $50,000 per annum! By this time two years I can so arrange all my business as to secure at least $50,000 per annum. Beyond this never earn—make no effort to increase fortune, but spend the surplus each year for benevolent purposes. Cast aside business forever, except for others.

Settle in Oxford and get a thorough education, making the acquaintance of literary men—this will take three years' active work—pay special attention to speaking in public. Settle then in London and purchase a controlling interest in some newspaper or line review and give the general management of it attention, taking a part in public matters, especially those concerned with education and improvement of the poorer classes.

Man must have an idol—the amassing of wealth is one of the worst species of idolatry—no idol more debasing than the worship of money. Whatever I engage in I must push inordinately: therefore should I be careful to choose that life which will be the most elevating in its character. To continue much longer overwhelmed by business cares and with most of my thoughts wholly upon the way to make more money in the shortest time, must degrade me beyond hope of permanent recovery. I will resign business at thirty-five, but during the ensuing two years I wish to spend the afternoons in receiving instruction and in reading systematically.

This memo did not come to light until long after Carnegie's death, some 50 years later. More than anything else it shows a man divided against himself. He loves the success he had made of himself in the business world yet feels contempt for that very achievement. He is full of self-conscious virtue and promises himself to put aside his worldly gains and to devote the rest of his life to doing good for others.

Knowing what came next in his life, was he hypocritical? Perhaps he did mean what he wrote. Remember that, unlike many other business leaders of his time, his family in Dunfermline had long been fighters for social and economic justice. Yet the program for his future so nobly outlined was quickly forgotten. Instead of retiring in 2 years, he went on for 33 more. He rushed ahead to pile up greater and greater wealth until he became the richest man in the world. One of his biographers called him "the greediest little gentleman ever created."

The records show that this was one side of him. It is what makes Carnegie and people like him so interesting. As another historian said, "We see the unequal struggle between a man who loved money—loved making it, having it, spending it—and a man who, at bottom, was ashamed of himself for his acquisitive desires."

In the early postwar years Carnegie held major interests in companies that made iron products. Their output went mostly into projects of his Keystone Bridge Company. The advantages of steel over iron—its combination of strength and durability—were known long before the 19th century. But until the 1860s no one had figured out how to make steel efficiently. Steel is a mixture of pure (wrought) iron and a small amount of carbon. But great difficulties in combining the two made large-scale operations impossible.

Keeping up with new technological developments, Carnegie became excited by reports of a new steel production method that Henry Bessemer in England and William Kelly in America had discovered independently, around the same time. The process called for making steel out of pig iron by blowing cold air through the molten iron. It cut radically the cost of labor and machinery needed. Improvement on that process was soon made by a British inventor, William Siemens, creator of the "open hearth" method. This permitted the use of ores unworkable by the Bessemer process and produced a more uniformly high quality of steel.

American producers quickly seized on the innovative processes and soon led the world in applying them. Steel became the basic metal of modern industry.

From experiments in his own mill with the new process, Carnegie concluded he could make durable rails of uniform quality at a price low enough for the railroad companies to accept. But he needed the right kind of iron ore in quantity enough to meet the expected demand. Just at the right moment the rich iron ore fields in Michigan's Upper Peninsula were opened up. The iron was the purest and most easily extracted to be found anywhere in the world. Carnegie decided that rather than convert his old iron plants for steel production, he would build a completely new mill with the best and latest equipment.

From making iron products Carnegie turned to the new process of making steel, the basic metal of modern industry.

But what about his many other interests, in telegraph lines, in sleeping cars, in railroads? He gradually turned away from them to concentrate all his efforts on one enterprise—the making of steel. He committed himself to "putting all his eggs in one basket, and then watching that basket."

A number of circumstances caused this switch. For one thing, there was the gamble involved in starting a new enterprise. He knew how often the outcome of an enterprise or investment depended upon luck. He had known much good luck but had met bad luck too. Some of his ventures failed and ended up in bitter disputes and shattered friendships.

The most painful example was the wreckage of his long and intimate relationship with Tom Scott. Carnegie had induced Scott to make some investments that turned out badly. Their friendship cooled. Then, in the panic that began in 1873, Scott faced the worst financial crisis of his life, and came to his old white-haired boy, Andy, for help. Carnegie refused him. The break became complete and permanent.

Such sad outcomes were less likely to occur, Carnegie believed, if he devoted himself to a single enterprise. So steel became his all-consuming passion.

As steel proved to be cheaper, stronger, and more durable than iron, new uses and new demands for it opened up rapidly. Bridge builders turned to steel-cable suspension designs, and architects such as Louis Sullivan turned to steel for the construction of the nation's first high-rise buildings—the skyscrapers. The railroads consumed millions of tons of the new material every year as they built new lines across the country. And countless people bought steel products for everyday use—wire, nails, bolts, needles, screws.

A steelmaker at that time with any brains couldn't help but expand. Carnegie of course had the brains—more than most. Without him, the Carnegie Steel Company would never have become the largest such firm in the world and one of the biggest businesses in all American industry.

Carnegie had not only had brains, but also experience. From his years on the railroad he had learned the concept of control. The railroads by this time had perfected a system of reports and directives, moving upward and downward in the structure. Everyone from the top manager to the bottom workers knew what was expected of him, what he would have to accomplish it with, and how and by whom his results would be judged. The individual was never lost sight of. Every day each man had to use his common sense and his skills to carry out his tasks and to make sure they meshed with the tasks of others.

To site his new steel mill, Carnegie got hold of 100 acres of land about 12 miles south of Pittsburgh, on the Monongahela River. He induced several friends and his

Carnegie steel went into erecting the nation's first high-rise buildings—the skyscrapers.

brother, Tom, to invest in the construction of the plant, holding the major share for himself. It was the first large-scale, integrated steel mill. He named it the Edgar Thomson Works, after his old boss, the head of the Pennsylvania. Of course he knew he must depend on Thomson's railroad, as well as others, to purchase his chief product, steel rails, and for the best rates to bring in his raw materials and to carry them out to the market.

But there was more than flattery behind the adoption of Thomson's name. The man was a self-taught engineer who made himself a hero of that profession. He was brilliant in planning, construction, and operation of the Pennsylvania. His appetite for taking in every new idea, every technical advance in railroading, could never be satisfied. The example he set as a most daring entrepreneur fired Carnegie's imagination.

Although there were a few steel mills doing business well before Carnegie came along, he didn't worry. He would learn from their mistakes. And by introducing the latest and most efficient equipment he would undersell the competition.

Just as construction began on his giant new steel mill, the economy toppled. In September 1873 the banking house of Jay Cooke collapsed. Down came hundreds of other banks and businesses. Panic spread swiftly. Men, women, and children vanished suddenly from the long aisles of the textile mills. Miners climbed out of the earth and left gaping holes for years to come. Farmers walked out of their fields, and the plows rusted alone.

That depression was one of the biggest and worst. It grew deeper and deeper and by 1877 had engulfed all but the rich.

What brought it on? In their race for profits, investors poured money recklessly into mines, mills, and railroads. They spent huge sums of capital on projects that could not bring returns for years to come. Eager to keep profits high, businesses overproduced in every market while squeezing workers' wages to the lowest possible level. Employers pocketed the profits instead of sharing them with labor through higher wages and lower hours, or they plowed profits back into still more production. The great mass of people lacked the buying power that the national economy needed to maintain its prosperity.

Iron mills and steel works that had expanded in the postwar prosperity could find no markets and had to stop production and lay off workers. Yet Carnegie would not cry halt to his new project. The ruin of so many hopes was visible all around him. Still, it did not discourage him. His partners croaked doom; he pushed ahead. His optimistic faith in America's long-term prosperity never wavered. He saw the depression as temporary; the economy would recover and soar even higher. Shrewdly he took advantage of the terrified business firms from whom he would purchase the equipment for his new mill. He bought at greatly reduced prices. And he hired unemployed workers at greatly reduced wages.

Everything was set to go—plant, supervisors, workers. All Carnegie had to do was sell his products. And to supervise supervisors. That was his most important task. He followed the practice he had introduced in earlier enterprises: tie the best man to the business, not by paying the highest salaries but by giving them a share in the business. That share could be tiny—a fraction of 1 percent. It was enough, however, to eventually make them millionaires in their own right.

In August 1875 the Thomson steelworks got its first order: 2,000 steel rails, from, of course, the Pennsylvania Railroad. Making tough, strong, malleable, and cheap rails was what the American steel industry was all about in those years. That was the beginning of Carnegie's steel empire. It would grow spectacularly over the next 30 years. Partly because of what every successful business of that time was doing. They expanded by acquiring other enterprises, or by merging with them. They formed trade alliances (like to Bessemer Steel Association) to exchange information and lobby for high tariffs to protect their products from foreign competition. They made secret agreements to fix prices, agreements that almost always collapsed when one company would double-cross the others by suddenly lowering prices. Carnegie, the best low-cost producer in the industry, was a master at such operations.

The casting crew working on an open-hearth platform in Carnegie's new Edgar Thomson Works. No safety equipment was provided.

He was a master too at the way he structured his business. He coordinated all aspects of production and distribution by vertically integrating his business. Wanting his own sources of raw materials, he acquired iron ore, coke, and coal fields and developed a fleet of steamships and a railroad for transporting materials directly to his steel mills. He was no longer dependent on suppliers, which meant he never paid a price, profit, or royalty to outsiders. He used his control of oil fields to pressure railroads into cutting the rates they charged for hauling his oil. And he bullied them into giving him kickbacks on the inflated rates they charged his competitors.

To design and supervise the building of the Thomson works, Carnegie had chosen Alexander L. Holley. The greatest American authority on the Bessemer process, Holley was a multitalented man whose inventive genius enhanced any enterprise he touched. Holley's plan for the works provided for the ready handling of inbound and outbound trains of three railroads. Being able to cheaply transport supplies coming in and products going out was the basis of his whole design. Holley brought along with him Captain Bill Jones, a Civil War veteran with a vast practical knowledge of the new craft of steelmaking. Jones perfected both process and machinery and contributed enormously to the success of Carnegie's steel empire.

Jones had his reward for such service. When Carnegie offered to make him a partner with the usual small share he gave his top management, Jones refused. Instead, he said, he wanted "a hell of a big salary." Asked to name his price, he answered tentatively, "15,000 a year?" He did better. Carnegie gave him $25,000—same pay drawn by the president of the United States.

Jones had started with Carnegie as a ten-dollar-a-day mechanic. But if any one person deserves the credit for making the Thomson works the best in the industry, it was Jones. He built it, managed it, improved it. His inventive genius earned him more major patents than any other person in the history of steel. He also made hundreds of improvements in the design, construction, and operation of machinery which he though were too minor to patent.

To Carnegie, Jones was the indispensable man. Then one night in the fall of 1889, a new blast furnace in the Thomson works exploded. Jones, standing nearby, leaped backward and fell to the plant's lower level. His head hit the side of an ore car, knocking him unconscious. Two days later he died the accidental death that took the lives of so many steelworkers.

Scarcely two days after Jones's funeral, Carnegie's lawyers convinced his distraught and grieving widow to sell the company all Jones's patent rights for the sum of $35,000. It was a trifling payment for the invaluable patents.

Bill Jones was but one of the brilliant young men with whom Carnegie surrounded himself. Another was Henry Clay Frick, the son of German-Swiss immigrants who was born in 1849 in western Pennsylvania. His sole desire when growing up was to become rich like his grandfather, who made a famous brand of rye whiskey. Small and slight of build, Frick was a cold and inflexible personality. In his school years he cared only about mathematics, believing it

As the depression of the 1870s deepened and government provided no relief for the starving, private charity tried to help with soup kitchens for the poor.

73

would help him in business. For a few years he was a sales-
man in a department store. Then, at 21, he began to climb
when he bought a share in 123 acres of coke lands in his
own farm region. Knowing how vital the coking process
was to steel production, he began to expand his holdings
considerably. He survived the 1873–78 depression by
extensive borrowing and the use of the same kind of "honorable tricks" that helped make Carnegie rich. By the time
the economic crisis was over, he controlled Pennsylvania's
high-grade coke fields and had earn himself the title "Coke
King." With steel production going full blast and demand
for coke shooting up, he kept raising the price of his coke.
By the time he was 30 he was a millionaire.

Frick's biggest customer, Andrew Carnegie, admired
his "positive genius" in management. In 1883 Carnegie
drew Frick into his embrace by buying a half-share in the
coke company. "Efficiency" was Frick's motto, as it was
Carnegie's; he let nothing human stand in his way. The
combination of the Carnegie and Frick companies was of
great benefit to both. In 1889 Frick became general manager of the whole enterprise. Under his forceful hand the
annual output of the Carnegie works rose tenfold.

Just as important to Carnegie was Charles Schwab. His
grandfather had come from Germany to America in 1830.
In 1879, at 17, young Schwab took a job in the Carnegie
works as a lowly stake driver at a dollar a day. Six months
later Bill Jones asked him to supervise the construction of a
new blast furnace. It was a great success, and Carnegie
himself asked to see the young man. Like Jones, he was
captivated by Charlie's charm. His ability to sing, play the
piano, juggle, and joke made him a happy contrast to the
grim Frick.

With only a sketchy high school education, Schwab
taught himself enough engineering so that he could design
and build a railroad bridge and bring it under the estimated cost. He gathered technical books, studied them, creat-

Bill Jones, Charles Schwab, and Henry Clay Frick—three men whose inventive genius and managerial talents contributed much to Carnegie's success in steel production

ed a laboratory in his own house, and mastered the chemistry of metallurgy.

At the age of 25, Schwab became superintendent of Carnegie's steel plant in Homestead. And two years later, when Bill Jones was killed, Schwab was made the new chief superintendent of the Thomson works. While he lacked Jones's intuitive feel for the making of steel, he knew much more about its science. Unlike Jones, he was no maverick and always did what Carnegie wanted. Everybody loved him, it was said, including the workers, except when it was time to go out on strike.

In 1881 Carnegie consolidated all his holdings—steelworks, coke works, iron mills, furnaces, coal mines. He named the business Carnegie Bros. & Company, Ltd. Tom Carnegie was made chairman of the board, and besides the two brothers, there were only five other shareholders.

Oddly, Carnegie himself held no official position in the company. Titles, he said, meant "simply nothing" to him.

But he had 55 percent of the capital.

EIGHT

THE SACRED RIGHT
TO ORGANIZE

Carnegie was a ruthless manager of his workmen. His relentless concern for costs drove his men to produce more and more without getting any reward in the form of higher pay. It was said he never wanted to know the profits but always wanted to know the costs. His motto was "watch the costs, and the profits will take care of themselves." "Cut costs! Cut costs!" was the hammering refrain in his mills. It was behind his readiness to mechanize production, to introduce the newest equipment, to streamline operations.

That drive for economy, said the labor historian David Brody, "finally defined the treatment of steel workers. Long hours, low wages, bleak conditions, anti-unionism, flowed alike from the economizing drive that made the American steel industry the wonder of the manufacturing world."

To Carnegie wages were especially bothersome. He tried his best to cut the cost of labor per ton of finished steel. He kept a close watch on what the competition was paying its workers. In a note to one of his executives he wrote that a competitor was paying "but sixty cents a day for labor and that the result is better than when they gave two dollars."

Of course this was not better for the workers: it was better for profits. The only man in the plant who stood up to Carnegie on this issue had been Bill Jones. He was as fiercely competitive as Carnegie but refused to cut wages below a certain minimum. "Our men are working hard and faithfully," he said, when Carnegie asked for further cuts. "Our labor is the cheapest in the country. Leave good enough alone."

Those words didn't mean that Jones and Carnegie went easy on their workers. The men put in 12-hour shifts, seven days a week, including Sundays, even in summertime, when the thermometer inside soared above 100 degrees. When local clergy protested the breaking of the Sabbath, Jones told them to keep their noses out of his business. If they didn't, he would fire every worker who went to their church. The only holiday the mill respected was the Fourth of July.

Within the mill, Carnegie's policies fostered the most intense competitive spirit. The blast furnaces were pitted against each other in quantity of production. The one that did best each week had a giant steel broom hoisted high on its smokestack, proclaiming to Pittsburgh who the mightiest men in town were. Without it costing him an extra penny in wages, Carnegie incited the men to drive themselves as though they were competing for an Olympic gold medal.

It took a long time before American workmen tried to defend themselves by organizing trade unions. Partly it was because the employers were so strong and clung so tightly to their antiunion position. But the public too was slow in appreciating the need for collective action by labor. People's views were shaped by America's individualistic tradition. And finally, most local, state, and federal governments in that era were against unions.

Even within the ranks of labor itself there were strong factors that slowed down union organization. Many workers came into the factories with the same individualistic attitude held by the general public. They believed in the success myth, in the model of the Horatio Alger stories. You made it on your own, or you weren't worth much. They clung to dreams of some day having their own shops or companies. The few like Carnegie, who did make it on their own, got enormous publicity and praise. The anonymous millions who were never able to raise their heads much above poverty were forgotten.

And then there was the influence of prejudice. The labor force contained African-Americans, immigrants (one-third of all industrial workers in 1870 were foreign born), women, and children. These groups were often ignored or discriminated against by the unions. Immigrants were occasionally used by employers as scabs, and so were African-Americans.

Even when the various unions plunged into the hard task of organizing mines, mills, and whole industries, they often differed among themselves on goals, on strategy, on tactics. There was no central unifying force that might have made their task somewhat less difficult and painful. What did those unions want? Some of them didn't fully accept industrial capitalism. They hoped to raise their members into the self-employed class, into a middle-class status, by forming cooperative factories. Then the workers would no longer be hired hands but working for themselves and for one another.

Another current of thought in the labor movement was revolutionary: industrialism, yes, but capitalism, no. These socialist, or Marxist, unions wanted to end the exploitation of workers by employers. They called for turning the means of production over to the people who did the work, either directly to them or to them through their own elected government.

Never large in number, the radical unions frightened the employers and the public by their declared readiness to use violence, if necessary, to overthrow the system of private ownership of property. Their radical propaganda probably made employers somewhat more ready to deal with conservative unions.

The nonradical unions wanted to negotiate with employers. They relied on persuasion, education, and legislation to gain their goals. But when workers met with employers who denied their right to organize, refused to negotiate, turned a deaf ear to persuasion or education, and pressured government to pass antilabor legislation, they felt their only recourse was to strike.

Carnegie's first conflict with a union occurred in 1867. The iron puddlers throughout the Pittsburgh region had organized a small craft union called the Sons of the Vulcan. They refused to accept an industrywide cut in wages and went on strike, at Carnegie's iron mill as well as others.

The first great collision between capital and labor came in the Railway Strike of 1877. In labor's rebellion against wage cuts and blacklists, 100 people were killed. Federal and state troops broke the strike.

Rather than negotiate with the union, the iron bosses pooled funds to import foreign workers to take the jobs of the strikers.

Carnegie would use every device to overcome labor's pressure to make a decent living. He would needle his plant managers and department heads to hire fewer men, reduce hourly wages, and where possible replace human labor with machinery. He would ask rival firms to tell him what their labor costs were, and if they resisted him, he bribed their foremen into giving him the figures.

He would then go to Bill Jones and try to convince him to agree to wage reductions. Jones was too valuable a man for Carnegie to ignore his opinions. And Jones believed in paying the men a living wage for the terribly hard and dangerous work they did. It was Jones who persuaded Carnegie to give up the traditional two-shift 12-hour workday and go to the three-shift, 8-hour schedule in the Thomson works. Jones argued that men working 8 hours a day would be more productive and less tired than those on a 12-hour shift. The new schedule would also reduce absenteeism and the high rate of costly accidents.

Carnegie reluctantly gave in to this radical innovation and then proudly boasted of how enlightened he was in his labor policy. He was torn between two desires that were hard to reconcile. He wanted above all to reduce labor costs so that his steel mills could outdo his competitors in profit making. Yet he also wanted to present himself to the world as America's most liberal, most enlightened industrialist. Bill Jones argued that a humane labor policy was good business practice, that he could even make more money by it. But playing just as great a role was Carnegie's memory of his radical Scottish heritage. In making himself a multimillionaire, the employer of tens of thousands of workers, had he betrayed the faith of his fathers?

To justify himself, in April 1886 Carnegie published an article in *Forum*, a national magazine. Painting a rosy picture, he said that the conflict between capital and labor would disappear as management gradually came to accept peaceful cooperation with the trade union movement:

> *The right of the working man to combine and to form trades-unions is no less sacred than the right of the manufacturer to enter into associations and conferences with his fellows, and it must be sooner or later conceded. . . . My experience has been that trades-unions upon the whole are beneficial both to labor and capital.*

He then suggested that employers adopt a sliding-scale plan in paying wages, a plan that he would install in all his own plants:

> *What we must seek is a plan by which the men will receive high wages when their employers are receiving high prices for the product, and hence are making large profits; and per contra, when the employers are receiving low prices for products, and therefore small if any profits, the men will receive low wages.*

The article was understood by the labor movement as a Magna Carta, given freely by the King of Steel. But industry leaders hated it. The article appeared just when the labor movement was battling for an eight-hour day throughout the country. The unions had set May 1, 1886, as the date for nationwide strike if the eight-hour day had not been granted to all workers. Chicago's workers demonstrated with a peaceful parade on that day. But on May 3, Chicago police tangled with striking workers at the McCormick Harvester plant. As strikebreakers were leaving the shop gates, the strikers flung sticks and stones. Police rushed up with clubs and guns. Four workers were killed and several others wounded. A meeting to protest police brutality was called for the next night, in Haymarket Square.

Speaker after speaker took the stand until there was a

In 1886 strikes for the eight-hour day took place in industrial centers almost everywhere. In Chicago on May 3, police clashed with striking workers at the McCormick Harvester plant.

glaring red flash and a terrific explosion. A dynamite bomb had come out of nowhere and had hit the ground near the front rank of the police. Seven of them were fatally wounded and 67 others hurt. In the dark, police opened fire on the crowd. As people ran, the maddened police charged, clubbing and shooting. In a few seconds the square was red with blood. Ten workers fell dead and another 50 were wounded. The next day Chicago's press and the nation's screamed for revenge.

Carnegie rushed back into the pages of *Forum* with another article. He said the hysteria over the strike movement was way out of proportion. Only 250,000 out of 20 million workingmen had gone on strike, and he blamed management, not labor, for the strike. Owners should pay more attention to their workers' complaints, he said, and meet them more than halfway. But he also warned that the nation would not tolerate violence and lawlessness.

Then he added a passage strongly supporting the right of a worker to his job, lines that would indict him for hypocrisy in the years to come:

> *To expect that one dependent upon his daily wage for the necessaries of life will stand peaceably and see a new man employed in his stead is to expect much. . . . The employer of labor will find it much more to his interest, wherever possible, to allow his works to remain idle and await the results of a dispute than to employ a class of men that can be induced to take the place of other men who have stopped work. Neither the best men as men, nor the best men as workers, are thus to be obtained. There is an unwritten law among the best workmen: Thou shalt not take thy neighbor's job.*

He ended his article by complimenting labor leaders, including the head of the steel workers union. "Let no one be unduly alarmed by frequent disputes between capital and labor," he said. "Kept within legal limits, they are encouraging symptoms, for they betoken the desire of the working-man to better his condition; and upon this desire hang all the advancements of the masses."

What were the conditions that Carnegie said labor wanted to see improved?

It can't be denied that out of the great economic growth of the country in the post–Civil War era came an increase in real wages. Despite that fact, the average industrial worker did not earn enough to support a family decently. In 1890, steelworkers averaged about $450 a year. Women and children in factories earned much less. Race and nationality affected income too. European immigrants, blacks, and Chinese were slotted into the lowest-paying jobs.

Large numbers of workers remained desperately poor.

In Pennsylvania, coal miners struggled to support families on $200 a year or less. Their homes were rickety, unpainted shacks; their food, mush and potatoes. In Chicago thousands worked in sweatshops under appalling conditions, laboring endless hours almost for pennies. An Illinois study found that one out of every four workers "fail to make a living."

Only a tiny minority of unskilled workers ever achieved the kind of rags-to-riches climb the popular success literature claimed was common. One study of a Massachusetts factory town showed that from 1850 to 1880 few unskilled workers rose beyond the ranks of the semi-skilled, and almost none achieved middle-class status. The sons of manual laborers tended to become semiskilled workers. Poor men could improve their condition only by putting their wives and children to work and by rigid economizing. Still, nearly all remained in the laboring class.

No wonder the press noted the growing bitterness or working people. The industrial, technological wonders of the age were highly touted everywhere. But what had they delivered for the mass of workers?

In the last quarter of the 19th century there was an enormous gap between rich and poor, between the top and the bottom in American society. In 1890, the top 1 percent owned 51 percent of all property. The bottom 44 percent, just 1 percent. In the top group the families averaged $164,000 in wealth. In the bottom group, $150.

In Chicago, Marshall Field paid his best workers in his giant department store $12 for a 59-hour week. Mr. Field himself pocketed $600 every hour of the 24-hour day, every day of the 365-day year.

A New York newspaper reported in 1892 there were more than 4,000 millionaires in the country. They had so much money that some filled their teeth with diamonds and spent $75,000 for a pair of opera glasses and $65,000 for a dressing table. A pet poodle wore a diamond collar worth

$15,000, and a host offered his guests cigarettes wrapped in hundred-dollar bills.

Andrew Carnegie built himself a 64-room mansion on New York's Fifth Avenue. Many of the newly rich housed themselves in such palaces in imitation of the old European aristocracy.

AN "INNOCENT" ABROAD

One pleasure of growing rich Carnegie speedily learned. Once he made an investment, he did not have to remain on the scene to reap the profits. It was like magic. Money made more money. And early on Carnegie began to enjoy the benefits, taking long vacations, safe in the assurance that while he was gone, he would grow richer and richer.

But few businessmen did what he did. Instead they were tied to their executive chair, fearful of losing touch, hesitant to leave others in charge. Carnegie prided himself on not devoting his every hour to business. Unlike the great majority of the industrial moguls he did not limit his interests to the profit-and-loss sheet. He preferred to have good books to read and the best-educated people to talk with. And his circle did not include the idle rich of high society who had nothing to say except social gossip. As time went on, he would often spend as much as half the year away from work, traveling, savoring new experiences, meeting old friends—experiencing life in all its rich variety.

His first extended holiday, with his mother, had been to his birthplace in Scotland, in 1862. The three months abroad had been spoiled by a siege of pneumonia that lasted six weeks.

Three years later, with two of his friends, Carnegie visited England, France, and Germany, a trip that made him "very fond of the Germans," he said. "It is all wrong that a people like the French should be allowed to control matters to so great an extent."

He was a tireless tourist, ticking off cities and countries and monuments and museums and theaters and opera houses in the guidebooks. But he also never neglected to look into new manufacturing processes of possible value to his own enterprises. He was quick to negotiate for the American rights to any foreign-held patents of interest to him. Of course he sought out important businessmen he might eventually buy from or sell to.

During his nine months abroad, Carnegie placed the burden of safeguarding his business interests at home on his 22-year-old brother, Tom. His frequent letters to Tom were full of advice—do this, do that, don't do this, don't do that—implying that Tom, after all, wasn't as smart as his big brother. The truth was, Tom was well qualified to take care of the Carnegie interests and knew a great deal about all of them. He was better liked both by their partners and their workers; they both trusted him more. Lacking Andrew's relentless drive, Tom would never have been able to build the steel empire, but he was well-fitted to take care of what Andrew achieved.

In the fall of 1878, Carnegie and one companion began a five-month trip around the world. He later said it opened up a new horizon for him and changed his intellectual outlook. He became deeply interested in the writings of Charles Darwin and Herbert Spencer and began to view life from the standpoint of evolutionism. He held, like Spencer, that evolution guaranteed progress toward perfection. "All is well since all grows better." This was a comfortable creed for a wealthy man to live by.

Despite the burden of what he considered to be superstitious religion, he concluded that "the masses of all nations are usually happy." Even the poverty-stricken tapioca workers he saw in southeast Asia, the parents working stark naked, and the children running about in rags. "If all is not well," he wrote, "yet all is coming well. In this faith we find peace. The endless progress of the race is assured now that evolution has come with its message and shed light where before there was darkness, reassuring those who thought and who therefore doubted most."

Finally, his experience made him aware of another advantage to be had from viewing so many different peoples and cultures:

> *The sense of the brotherhood of man, the unity of the race, is very greatly strengthened thereby, for one sees that the virtues are the same in all lands, and produce their good fruits, and render their possessors blessed . . . that the vices too are akin, and also that the motives which govern men and their actions and aims are very much the same the world over. In their trials and sufferings, as in their triumphs and rejoicings, men do not differ, and so the heart swells and the sympathies extend, and we embrace all men in our thoughts, leaving not one outside the range of our solicitude and wishing every one well.*

Three years later, in June 1881, Carnegie took his mother and a group of nine friends on a trip in Great Britain. Getting off the steamer, they traveled in a splendid big coach drawn by four horses from the southern coastal town of Brighton in England to Inverness in Scotland, 831 miles away, and then grandly into Carnegie's hometown, Dunfermline. They arrived at four in the afternoon, rolling in under banners reading "Welcome Carnegie, generous son" to meet an applauding crowd of eight thousand people.

Of course they stopped in front of the little stone house

Carnegie enjoyed many long vacations abroad. In 1881 he took his mother and nine friends on a coaching trip in Great Britain. He stands, whip in hand, with his mother beside him.

where Andy had been born. Then Carnegie had the extraordinary pleasure, before his mother and all the townfolk, of laying the cornerstone of a free public library.

But not all of the tour of his native land was so enjoyable. He criticized the British monarchy, the established church, and the gap between the rich and the poor, which had not narrowed since his radical forebears had assailed it. Although his own steel mills were polluting the air of Pittsburgh, he nevertheless criticized the textile mills for making a mess of England's industrial midlands. Yet he noted that "the working classes in England do not work so hard or so unceasingly as their fellows in America. They have ten holidays to America's one." Americans, he added, are "the saddest looking race" he had ever seen. "Life is so terribly earnest. . . . Ambition spurs us all on, from him who handles the spade to him who employs thousands. We know no rest." "We?" Carnegie? Or the steelworkers he had putting in 84 hours a week?

Meanwhile, during all these vacations abroad, it was brother Tom who took care of business. He had been made chairman of the steelworks. In his letters home Andrew dealt with him just as he did with other supervisors. He made harsh remarks about his performance and outrageous putdowns and then sugared it with emotional pep talks or hollow flattery. He kept telling Tom he knew he was imposing a heavy burden upon him, "but if you succeed it will be a lasting benefit to you."

Benefit? In the end it destroyed Tom. He handled his responsibilities very well, everyone close to the business said. But he never felt the passion for it that drove his brother. Though a good businessman, he was not an aggressive competitor. In the early 1880s he took to drinking heavily. In October 1886 it killed him. Like his father, he seemed to have lost all desire to live. He was 40 years old. He left a wife, nine children, and a fortune.

As Tom sank into his final illness, Andrew fell sick too. He almost died of typhoid. Before he recovered, his mother, Margaret Carnegie, caught pneumonia, and within weeks of Tom's passing, she too died, in November 1886. She was 76.

Five months later, Carnegie married Louise Whitfield. He was 51, and she was 23.

Marrying so soon after his mother's death did not occur by chance. The timing of that marriage casts light upon Carnegie's relationship with his mother. He had taken his mother with him some 20 years before when he moved from Pittsburgh to New York. They lived in luxurious suites in various hotels. To escape the heat of summers in the city, from early June to late October they would move into the summerhouse Carnegie built at Cresson, Pennsylvania, high up in the Allegheny Mountains, about

50 miles east of Pittsburgh. The pollution of his steel mills below in the valleys did not dirty the pure air of his summer retreat.

Although surrounded by servants to do her bidding, Margaret was never content unless Andrew was there to pay her lots of attention. Her younger son, with his rapidly growing young family, had no need of her emotionally and escaped from her strangling embrace. If Andrew ever hinted that he might like some time on his own, his mother instantly said no, this was as good as life could get. She seemed never to fear he would rebel and set her aside, to claim his personal independence. Nor did he show any real desire to do it.

Carnegie had many young girlfriends as the years went by. But it was always just as friends, not lovers. Several at a time would be invited, properly chaperoned, especially by Mrs. Carnegie, to Cresson, and some were escorted in groups on Carnegie junkets to Europe.

But in 1880, with Carnegie 45 and his mother nearing 70, she saw the first real threat to her place in her son's life. He met young Louise Whitfield, the daughter of a prosperous New York merchant. Her family lived near Carnegie's hotel. Carnegie met them through a mutual friend. He owned fine horses and was accustomed to taking young women riding with him in Central Park. Soon the shy but attractive Louise became part of the group. "In the end the others faded into ordinary beings," Carnegie said. "Miss Whitfield remained alone as the perfect one beyond any I had met." Louise, tall (three inches taller than Andrew), graceful, handsome rather than pretty, was not only a good rider but a serious thinker whose conversation Carnegie enjoyed.

In planning his 1881 coaching trip to Britain, Carnegie invited Louise to join the party. She was delighted but worried that her mother (her father had died a few years before) might not think it proper. So to calm her mother's fears, Carnegie asked his own mother to urge Mrs. Whitfield to let Louise accept by assuring her there would be proper chaperonage.

Andrew's intense concern that Louise join the coaching party strengthened his mother's growing suspicion that this was not a casual relationship. She didn't mind that at least three other young women had agreed to go. But Louise worried her. Still, she put on her best afternoon dress and called on the Whitfields to extend the formal invitation that Louise join them. "But is it quite proper for an unattached young lady to accept?" asked Mrs. Whitfield. "What would you do if you were in my place?"

Margaret Carnegie barked out her ready answer. "If she were a daughter of mine she wouldn't go!"

That settled it. The miserably disappointed Louise didn't go. She never forgave Mrs. Carnegie. And long after, late in life, talking with one of Carnegie's biographers, she said that Mrs. Carnegie "had been the most unpleasant person she had ever known."

After Carnegie returned from Scotland his friendship with Louise picked up again. But her feelings about him were mixed. Would he ever marry while his mother remained alive? And how long would this strong old lady live? Then too, did she really want to marry a man twice her age, a man nearly as old as her mother? What kind of marriage could it be? He was enormously rich, this steel king, and unlike a young lover, did not need a mate to help him get started on the road to success. After all, he had got along without a wife all these years. Did he need a wife now? Or would he feel the loss of freedom he plainly enjoyed when single?

Putting all these questions aside, they got secretly engaged in September 1883. It was a troubled engagement. Six months later, by mutual agreement, they broke it off. But neither was happy about that, so they became engaged once again. Now the question was, when would they

Carnegie, with his wife, Louise Whitfield. When they married in 1887, he was 51, and she 23.

marry? Louise was convinced Andrew would never marry while his mother lived, for he couldn't bring himself to defy his mother's wishes. That Louise put up with it so patiently, if painfully, reveals the depth of her feelings.

But at last, when Margaret was gone, Andrew and Louise were free to marry. It was an informal wedding, on April 22, 1887, with only 30 people present—family and close friends. For a wedding gift Carnegie gave his bride a large house in Manhattan at 5 West 51 Street and securities that would bring her an income of $20,000 a year. Then they left on a wedding trip to England.

TEN

BLOODY
HOMESTEAD

The extraordinary prolabor statements Carnegie had made in his 1886 *Forum* articles stunned and dismayed the other industrial leaders of his time. None of them thought this way. It was the labor leaders who showered him with compliments. One union even named a lodge after him, an honor that delighted him.

But to Frick, his right-hand man, his words were nonsense. Frick believed their companies were theirs to do with as they liked. They could hire anyone they chose, fire anyone they chose, pay whatever they chose.

A test of Carnegie's labor views came January 1, 1888, the day he posted at the Thomson works in Braddock his decision to end the 8-hour day and return to the 12-hour shift, and to introduce a sliding scale that would tie wages to steel prices.

He had learned that Chicago steel mills using the 12-hour shift were paying 6 percent less than he for crews of laborers. So he introduced new machinery in his own plant and prepared to return to the 12-hour shift.

The Thomson workers promptly put down their tools

and went home. Carnegie did not hire scabs to replace them. He shut down the mill and went home to New York. Negotiations to settle the dispute went nowhere. Carnegie insisted the men would work on his terms or not at all. Beaten down after five months without pay, the men voted to return to work. Carnegie had won. Now he would face his competitors with economies estimated at 19 percent against their previous advantage of 6 percent.

The next labor issue arose at Homestead, a completely modern steel mill a mile downriver from Braddock, which had been opened in 1881 by a group of Pittsburgh businessmen. But labor troubles became too much for the owners, and they sold out to Carnegie in 1883. When he took over the mill he had to deal with six highly organized labor lodges of the powerful Amalgamated Association of Iron and Steel Workers. Their determined campaign for a union contract tested the honesty of the prolabor attitude Carnegie had voiced in his *Forum* articles. Did he mean what he had said or was that just hot air? He passed the test. In 1889 he signed a three-year contract with the union, recognizing it as the sole bargaining agent for Homestead. This agreement angered Frick and his other partners and cost the company a slice of its profits.

The contract gave the skilled workers represented by the union wages that were one-third higher than those at neighboring steel mills. It also pegged the pay of the unorganized Homestead laborers to those of the skilled workers. So when the unionized workers won a major increase, it benefited the unskilled nonunion helpers as well. It gave all the workers at Homestead—craftsmen and laborer—a powerful common interest.

In Carnegie's mills in and around Pittsburgh, he employed over 14,000 common laborers to do the unskilled work. Nearly 12,000 of them were from southern and eastern Europe. Most earned less than $12.50 a week, at a time when a family needed $15 for bare subsistence. A staggering accident rate damaged these and other workers. In one year nearly 25 percent of the recent immigrants in one mill were injured or killed. So they had much to gain if they could come under the protection of the union.

The town of Homestead itself had only 11,000 residents, with 3,800 of them working in the steel mills. Steelworkers ran the town. They headed city government and the police force and owned most of the homes. They considered the union a natural right; it went along with citizenship. It was their guarantee against dependency. It protected a family's position as homeowner in the community they had made for themselves. They believed a steel mill created and run on their muscle and brains and blood was theirs as much as it was Carnegie's.

Step back a moment and look at what had been going on in the steel industry for some time. Skilled craftsmen played the major role in overseeing all phases of the complex production of steel. The mill owners reached per-ton and per-piece agreements with the skilled men. As these craftsmen organized, their unions began to negotiate those arrangements on a collective basis.

But new technologies came in rapidly, with industrialists like Carnegie making big investments in automated processes that reduced the need for skilled workers. The steel companies began to hire immigrants to tend the new machinery under the eye of salaried supervisors.

Finally, and most important, steel executives like Henry Frick made no pretense of cozying up to labor. They openly declared war to break the power of the strong craft unions. As unions nationwide suffered one defeat after another from the 1870s to the early 1890s, any hesitancy about smashing labor once and for all vanished. Carnegie, spending less and less time near his mills, found ease of mind—and conscience—in letting Frick do the face-to-face dealing with labor. Now he, like Frick, wanted a compliant labor force, willing to work for low wages. To get it, they had to break the union.

Mill workers outdoors at lunchtime, from a painting by Thomas Anshutz. Carnegie's crews worked a 12-hour, seven-day shift, with but one day off during the year.

The partners agreed on a two-point plan, with Carnegie placing no limits on how Frick should manage the negotiations. The first aim was to reduce the pay. A new scale was pegged to $23 a ton, which meant a wage cut of 18 to 26 percent.

The second part was even worse, much worse: Bust the unions. At the right moment they would announce that all the employees "will be necessarily Non-Union after the expiration of the present agreement." They had the gall to say, this action "is not taken in any spirit of hostility to labor organizations." In Carnegie's own words, the "democratic" justification for breaking the union was that "as the vast majority of the employees are non-union [the unskilled workers] the minority must give place to the majority."

After agreeing to this plan, Carnegie and his beloved Louise sailed off on a long vacation in Scotland. Behind him he left Frick, eager to do the dirty work. On his arrival Carnegie sent Frick a note: "We will approve of anything you do. We are with you to the end."

Although the hated Frick was alone in the seat of power, the Homestead workers approached the renewal of the contract with confidence. Carnegie was the major partner in the mill, wasn't he? Wouldn't he rein in Frick? But anticipating a shutdown at Homestead, he had already made arrangements to shift orders for steel to mills at Braddock and Duquesne.

Negotiations began in February 1892. Steel prices were booming, and the union asked for a raise. Frick's reply was to propose a wage cut. Negotiations dragged on. In June, Frick announced the company would deal with workers on an individual basis and would not renew its contract with the Amalgamated union. He knew the union could never accept that. So he prepared for battle, building three miles of a 12-foot-high steel fence around the mill, cutting rifle slits in it and topping it with barbed wire. The steelworkers dubbed the plant Fort Frick and concluded the company meant to smash the union. Then Frick gave the men an ultimatum: settle on his terms in one month or the company would quit dealing with the union.

Angered, the men carried out a mock public hanging of Frick. With this as an excuse, he shut down the mill and locked out the workers 10 days before the contract was to end.

At a mass meeting the three thousand unskilled workers voted to stand solid with the eight hundred union men. Frick moved fast to bring in scabs. Earlier he had secretly hired Pinkerton men to study the grounds. Now he ordered three hundred Pinkerton guards to get through the picketline and take over the plant so that they could protect the scabs he wanted to hire.

The mood of the Homestead workers was voiced by John Fitch, a special investigator, in a report on the situation:

The Homestead men had been working in the mill at that place, many of them since it was first built. They had seen it grow from a small beginning to one of the finest and best equipped plants in the world. They were proud of that plant and proud of the part that they had had in its progress.

Fitch stressed the pride in workmanship felt by the laborers. While they were absorbed in the work and what it produced, the owners were chiefly concerned with the profits derived from labor's efforts. Fitch goes on:

Over the hills rising from the river were their cottages, many of them owned by the workingmen . . . and now these homes were in jeopardy. They could have gone back to work. . . . But that meant giving up their union . . . self-disenfranchisement. So when the Pinkerton men came, the Homestead steel workers saw in their approach an attempt at subjugation at the hands of unauthorized individuals. A mob of men with guns coming to take their jobs . . . to take away the chance to work, to break up their homes—that is what passed through the minds of the Homestead men that morning.

At three o'clock on that morning of July 6, 1892, the morning Fitch speaks of, two big barges slipped into the mouth of the Monongahela River. Through the thick fog the men crowded on the decks could see the lights of Pittsburgh gleaming from the shore. Uniforms were handed out and the men put them on. They were the standard Pinkerton outfit: slouch hat, metal-buttoned blouse, dark blue pants with light stripes down the sides. Some of the men sat on the crates packed with rifles, pistols, and ammunition. The others lay on the deck or stood at the rail, discussing the secret mission in tense whispers.

There were more than three hundred of them, picked up by recruiting agents in Chicago and New York. Most were jobless, some were criminals on the run, others Civil

War veterans or ex-policemen, the rest—men running the show—were experienced professionals of the Pinkerton National Detective Agency. For the past 40 years, Pinkertons—a private army—had been used by industrialists wherever there were strikes to be broken or unions to be smashed. By now the agency had 2,000 trained men and 30,000 reserves.

At 4 A.M. that morning a workers' patrol sighted the Pinkerton barges a mile below Homestead. Whistles screamed through the town, and 10,000 men, women, and children rushed down to the riverbank. The barges hit the beach at dawn. All along the river's edge the Pinkertons saw carbines, rifles, shotguns, pistols, revolvers, clubs, and stones in workers' hands. Wildly excited voices shouted to the Pinkertons to turn back. Some in the crowd thought one barge carried strikebreakers and the other Pinkerton guards.

An advance group of Pinkertons stepped forward with their Winchester repeaters. The gangplank went down, and they started to cross it to shore. A striker lay down upon it, barring the way with his body. As a Pinkerton tried to kick him aside, the striker pulled out a revolver and shot him in the thigh.

Firing began at once from both sides. The Pinkertons on the gangplank blasted into the crowd, shooting down several workers. From topside on the barges, rifle fire cut down 30 Homestead men at once, while from the bank the crowd kept up fire on the barges.

The battle went on for 13 hours, the guards shooting over the water and the workers from behind barricades of scrap metal they quickly threw up.

It was one of the bloodiest battles in American labor history. The final count was never certain, but it is estimated that some 20 Pinkertons and 40 strikers were shot. Seven Pinkertons and 9 strikers died. The plant itself was untouched. At five that afternoon, the Pinkertons put up a white flag and marched unarmed up the shore where they were beaten badly by enraged wives of the workers before the sheriff's men took over.

The next day the company told the press:

In this engraving from a photograph, Pinkertons are seen in the foreground, surrendering after a bloody 13-hour battle with Carnegie's workers at the Homestead steel mill. Moving up the shore, they encounter the enraged families of locked-out workers.

> *This outbreak settles one matter forever, and that is that the Homestead mill hereafter will never again recognize the Amalgamated Association nor any other labor organization.*

Did it scare the workers? Not most of them. They were optimistic. Hadn't they won the first battle? They settled down to finish the war. Their big worry now was the possible use of the state militia against them.

News of bloody Homestead shook the outside world. Unions sent messages of support to the locked-out men. In Pittsburgh one union insisted the city council give back Carnegie's gift of a million dollars for a free library because, they said, the money was tainted with the blood of workers.

The Homestead workers kept up their guard. They took care of their wounded, buried their dead, and watched for another invasion of Pinkertons. A few days later, not Pinkertons, but eight thousand members of the Pennsylvania National Guard suddenly took over town, pitching camp on a hill overlooking it. "We are here," said their commanding general, "to restore law and order."

They stayed for over three months, while the company brought in scab after scab until nearly two thousand were inside, operating the steel mill. For five long months the locked-out men had held firm. But finally the troops, the scabs, costly court actions, evictions from company houses, press attacks, and hunger became too much. The feeling grew they were doomed to lose.

Men began drifting away, getting other jobs. The unskilled workers whose jobs could more easily be filled by scabs voted to go back to work. A few days later, the skilled men organized in the union also voted to return to work.

The Homestead strike was broken. Frick cabled Carnegie: OUR VICTORY IS NOW COMPLETE AND MOST SATISFYING. DO NOT THINK WE WILL EVER HAVE SERIOUS LABOR TROUBLE

AGAIN. WE HAD TO TEACH OUR EMPLOYEES A LESSON AND WE HAVE TAUGHT THEM ONE THEY WILL NEVER FORGET. Carnegie wrote to Frick: LIFE WORTH LIVING AGAIN. CONGRATULATIONS ALL AROUND.

The defeat crushed the union in Homestead. Frick himself was on hand to watch the union men ask for their old jobs. Almost none got them back. They who had once been the cream of the plant—the skilled, the indispensable—saw their jobs filled by new men, swiftly trained to take the craftsmen's place. Mechanization of the mills made it easy—skill didn't count so much.

The industrywide blacklist kept the union men out of every steel mill. It was a great blow to the Amalgamated. In two years it lost half its national membership as one employer after another refused to deal with it. By 1910 it had only one contract with a small company. Not until the 1930s, when labor organization was protected by New Deal legislation, did a new steel union rise to lift the workers out of poverty and fear.

The defeat of the Homestead strike devastated the town. When the novelist Hamlin Garland visited it soon after, in 1893, he wrote:

> *The town was as squalid and unlovely as could well be imagined, and the people were mainly of the discouraged and sullen type to be found everywhere where labor passes into the brutalizing stage of severity. . . . Such towns are sown thickly over the hill-lands of Pennsylvania. . . . They are American only in the sense in which they represent the American idea of business.*

Another observer found the Homesteaders "cheerless almost to the point of sullenness. The atmosphere was at times heavy with disappointment and hopelessness."

The individual workers at Homestead paid the heaviest price for the strike. And many continued to pay it for the rest of their lives. Job, home, personal possessions—all were gone. The few who were able to get their jobs back found their pay cut as much as 60 percent. It was the lowest pay of any mill in the industry. While steel mills generally cut wages because of the 1893 depression, the average reduction was 14 percent, not the 60 percent Carnegie demanded.

The 12-hour shift, seven days a week, was now standard in the steel industry. Although Carnegie continued to build libraries, few workers were able to use them. One steel man said he wanted an education above all else, "but after my day's work, I haven't been able to study. After working 12 hours how can a man go to a library."

To make sure no union would take hold again in any Carnegie mill, the company hired a corps of labor spies. They operated secretly, among the other workers. Their job was to report any signs of trouble. If they saw a man loafing on the job, wasting material, or voicing critical comments about the company, they turned in his name. The worst offense they watched for was any move to organize a union. At one time in 1899, 40 men, all of them young, not veterans of the 1892 strike, were found to be organizing at Homestead to revive the Amalgamated union. All were promptly fired. That was the last attempt to organize any of his works as long as Carnegie dominated the company. That same year, 1899, Carnegie Steel reported profits of $21 million.

But what did his victory over the workers do to Carnegie? In his autobiography, written long after, he wrote: "Nothing I have ever had to meet in all my life, before or since, wounded me so deeply. No pangs remain of any wound received in my business career save that of Homestead. It was so unnecessary."

He goes on to give a mostly inaccurate account of what happened at Homestead. It is full of distortions, falsehoods, and omissions. He might better have skipped that chapter in his life, but he could hardly do it. Instead he tried to convince the public he had no responsibility for what happened at his steel mill.

Homestead did Carnegie's reputation no good. Newspapers, church leaders, and politicians condemned him, both in America and Great Britain. One of the most bitter denunciations, widely printed, appeared in the *St. Louis Post-Dispatch*:

> *Count no man happy until he is dead. Three months ago Andrew Carnegie was a man to be envied. Today he is an object of mingled pity and contempt. In the estimation of nine-tenths of the thinking people on both sides of the ocean he had not given the lie to all his antecedents, but confessed himself a moral coward. One would naturally suppose that if he had a grain of consistency, not to say decency, in his composition, he would favor rather than oppose the organization of trades-union among his own working people at Homestead. One would naturally suppose that if he had a grain of manhood, not to say courage, in his composition, he would at least have been willing to face the consequences of his inconsistency.*

> *But what does Carnegie do? Runs off to Scotland out of harm's way to await the issue of the battle he was too pusillanimous to share. A single word from him might have saved the bloodshed—but the word was never spoken. Nor has he, from the bloody day until this, said anything except that he had "implicit confidence in the managers of the mills."*

> *The correspondent who finally obtained this valuable information expresses the opinion that "Mr. Carnegie has no intention of returning to America at present." He might have added that America can well spare Mr. Carnegie. Ten thousand "Carnegie Public Libraries" would not compensate the country for the direct and indirect evils resulting from the Homestead lockout. Say what you will of Frick, he*

*is a brave man. Say what you will of Carnegie, he is a cow-
ard. And gods and men hate cowards.*

Out of Homestead came one of labor's best-known songs,
called "Father Was Killed by the Pinkerton Men."

"Twas in a Pennsylvania town not very long ago
Men struck against reduction of their pay.
The millionaire employer with philanthropic show
Had closed the work till starved they would obey.
They fought for home and right to live where they had toiled
so long,
But ere the sun had set some were laid low.
There're hearts now sadly grieving by that sad and bitter
wrong,
God help them for it was a cruel blow.
            CHORUS
God help them tonight in their hour of affliction
Praying for him whom they'll ne'er see again
Hear the poor orphans tell their sad story
"Father was killed by the Pinkerton men."
Ye prating politicians, who boast protection creed,
Go to Homestead and stop the orphan's cry,
Protection for the rich man ye pander to his greed,
His workmen they are cattle and may die.
The freedom of the city in Scotland far away
'Tis presented to the millionaire suave,
But here in Free America with protection in full sway
His workmen get the freedom of the grave.
            CHORUS

ELEVEN

PRIVATE INTEREST– OR PUBLIC GOOD?

Homestead is fascinating because of what it shows about America's greatest philanthropist. He acted directly against his own public support for trade unions by the violent and bloody smashing of the union in his steel mill.

But Homestead reveals more than Carnegie's personal story. It dramatizes a great issue of 19th century industrial America: the conflict between the pursuit of private interest and the defense of the public good. What right do individuals have to pile up unlimited wealth and privilege when it directly limits the right of other—and far, far more —individuals to enjoy security in their jobs and dignity in their homes? Do material progress and technological advance inevitably lead to a great amount of social and economic inequality in an America that has committed itself to democracy for all?

That issue was just as intense, and just as unresolved, all through the 20th century. And as America enters the 21st century, it is still with us. Millions of people—working class and middle class—see themselves displaced and disenfranchised as the economy is internationalized. They have no say in the movement of their workplace overseas, in the loss of jobs, or in the loss of income, while their employers make these crucial decisions by themselves and for themselves.

What about Andrew Carnegie himself? Where did the defeat of the union at Homestead leave him? His first big problem was the depression that began in 1893, the worst economic crisis in the country's history up to that time. He knew that American industry was already producing more than enough to meet demand. That was true of steel in particular. Of the 13 major rail mills established in his time, eight had failed; he took over two of them. But business got even worse: 642 banks failed and 16,000 businesses closed down. Carnegie told his partners to expect a struggle to get orders for their steel. He launched intensive price-cutting to undersell competitors and backed it with intensive cost-cutting. He hunted down the cheapest source for raw materials, he beat down transportation costs, he tried to open up new markets, and he developed new products.

If his plans for combating the depression of the 1890s were to succeed, Carnegie needed the wholehearted support of his associates. He drove them harder than ever. He followed what every one of them did almost daily. Produce—or get out! About 15 of his partners were forced out. Frick was the first to go. Carnegie removed him as chief operating executive of Carnegie Steel but to save face for him he gave him the honorary title of chairman of the board. Only Charlie Schwab remained of the old team. Winning Carnegie's full confidence ("You're a hustler!" Carnegie told him), he was appointed president.

The depression of 1893 lasted for years and was a bitter disaster for working people. When it struck there were about 13 million families in the United States. Of these, 11 million had an average income of $380 a year. The richest 1 percent enjoyed wealth greater than the total remaining 99 percent. Yet Carnegie, whose steel mills were then drawing a profit of about $25 million a year, defied any man to show him there were paupers in this country. From his palace on Fifth Avenue he could not see Potter's Field, where the bodies of one out of every ten people who died in Manhattan were dumped into mass graves.

Although poverty persisted, tycoons like Carnegie were able to accelerate the growth of industry. It made for such abundance that few thought the country's wealth could ever be exhausted. The rich kept getting richer and piling up the means to invest and become even richer. The corporations that their lawyers created soon dominated the oil, electrical, railroad, mining, and many other industries.

Some social critics asked whether the aim of these corporations was to provide plenty for all. Their answer was no. It was rather to provide super-abundance for the few. Monopolies, or trusts, were established by powerful busi-

"Bosses of the Senate," a cartoon by Keppler in the satiric weekly Punch, *depicts who wielded the real influence in government. Note the steel trust on the right.*

109

nessmen to control prices in any given industry and suppress competition.

Alarmed by such great economic power in the hands of a few, reformers warned that the corporate lords would dominate not only the workplace but the halls of government.

Could that trend be halted? Many people began to think so. Churchmen started to preach the "social gospel," as opposed to Carnegie's "gospel of wealth." They called on their fellow clergy to focus on social issues and work for reform. They said man should not be treated as a thing to produce more things and then flung aside without consideration of his human needs.

Many Americans were reading two books that had an enormous influence on popular thought. One was Henry George's *Progress and Poverty* (1879), a passionate portrait of hard times that went through a hundred editions and made millions of people concerned about the inequality in American life.

The other was Edward Bellamy's *Looking Backward* (1887), a utopian novel set in the year 2000. It showed what life could be like if the social, economic, and political systems were organized to eliminate poverty, disease, and corruption. Countless Americans read it and absorbed its lessons.

Then, in 1892, the year of the Homestead strike, the new Populist, or People's, Party was launched at a convention in Omaha, Nebraska. Its platform was designed to appeal to workers and farmers alike. The preamble to the platform declared:

> We meet in the midst of a nation brought to the verge of moral, political, and material ruin. . . . The fruits of the toil of millions are boldly stolen to build up colossal fortunes for a few, unprecedented in the history of mankind; and the possessors of these, in turn, despise the Republic and endanger

liberty. From the same prolific womb of governmental injustice we breed the two great classes – paupers and millionaires.

The charge was clear: the controlling influences dominating the old political parties have allowed the existing dreadful conditions to develop without serious effort to restrain or prevent them.

The new party's presidential candidate, James B. Weaver, a Civil War veteran from Iowa, got nearly a million votes that year. Grover Cleveland, a Democrat, was elected president, but the Populists elected governors in Colorado, Kansas, North Dakota, and Wyoming; sent 2 senators and 11 congressmen to Washington; and sat 354 representatives in 19 state legislatures.

In the next presidential election, 1896, William Jennings Bryan was the candidate of both the Democrats and the Populists. Carnegie and his partners made huge contributions of cash to the Republican Party. Its candidate was William McKinley, long a congressman from Ohio. The upper classes feared the rising anger of the workers, the farmers, the poor, and the unemployed over their failure to secure a just share of the productivity of the new industrial age.

The Republican campaign whipped up a frenzied fear of the coming "revolution" should Bryan win. It was a strategy coldly calculated to blind the public to the real issues. In November Bryan rolled up the biggest Democratic vote thus far recorded, 6.5 million. Yet it was not enough to overcome McKinley's 7 million. The Republicans gained control of both houses of Congress, a dominating majority they would hold until 1932, when Franklin D. Roosevelt restored the Democrats to power.

The Populist press in the 1890s began calling Carnegie and his fellow industrialists "robber barons." Some historians looking back on that era disagree. They say Carnegie and Rockefeller and Morgan and the others were not robber barons but "industrial statesmen." It was through their methods of consolidation and improvements that America had acquired the greatest industrial strength that the world had ever known.

Carnegie himself said the charge of robber baron was false because he had organized his industry so superbly that the general public could now buy his steel at an unbelievably low price. He was able to market a pound of solid steel for one cent. What more could anyone ask?

What he neglected to say was that his annual profits were so high that his cost for producing steel was obviously way below one cent a pound. So large had the gap become between his cost of production and the market price of steel that his annual profits in a period of five years had increased more than 500 percent.

It is also worth noting that the industrialization of the United States after the Civil War was carried out with a great waste of natural resources, manpower, and capital. If America's natural resources had not been so abundant, if immigrants had not flooded the country's shore in unheard-of numbers, if the nation's geographic position had not provided political and military security, one wonders if the cost would have been tolerable. Workers, too, were treated like any other abundant natural resource—burned out quickly with the same carelessness.

Carnegie, like any other conqueror leading armies—a Tamerlane, a Genghis Khan, a Caesar, an Alexander—was self-centered. He acted out of self-interest. He did not think of the consequences for society or for the nation when he made his decisions.

Yet he took pride in producing steel products of the best quality. Once he told Schwab, "We are not in for dollars. Fortunately you and I and all our partners have plenty. . . . We have pleasure in business, performing useful parts—this is our great reward."

This was not quite true. His desire for dollars and more dollars, profit and more profit, was a major motive in his business life. Everyone around him knew that. But there was something more. And that was the desire for power. A Carnegie or a Rockefeller wanted imperial power. They wanted to be emperors of steel or oil, ruling supreme, operating by their own code of law.

Did that mean they wanted no interference by government? Not when they could get government to act positively in support of or defense of their business interests. Carnegie paid for a mighty effective lobbyist in Washington, who drafted protective tariff laws in aid of the steel industry and then got a dutiful Congress, well-oiled by gifts, to pass them. So, too, did he get patent laws passed.

And, of course when labor rebelled and went on strike, it was comforting to Carnegie to be able to have the National Guard or federal troops intervene on his side, all in the name of preserving law and order and protecting the sacred right of private property. An indication of how closely bonded a steel king and a president could become was the appointment by President McKinley of Philander C. Knox, as attorney general. Knox had been the corporation lawyer for the Carnegie Steel Company.

Toward the end of the 19th century the national government began creating the military-industrial complex that President Eisenhower was to warn the country against some 60 years later. The U.S. Navy decided to add modern steel warships to its fleet, which meant big orders for the steel mills. Carnegie, an outspoken advocate of pacifism, was torn between that principle and his hunger for a huge order. At first he decided not to bid for supplying the steel armor plates. But soon his desire for profits took over, and he began making the armor plate. Then he did the same for the Russian navy.

He was able to make armor plate for the U.S. Navy at a

cost of $150 a ton, while charging the government $450 a ton—a neat profit of 300 percent, which of course, came out of the taxpayer's pocket.

Later, in 1893, the Carnegie company was investigated on charges of fraudulent practices made by four workers within the Homestead plant—"whistleblowers," as they are called now. The company was found guilty by a special naval board and was fined. Still, Carnegie continued to get contracts for armor plate from the government.

RICHEST MAN
IN THE WORLD

In 1898 Carnegie was 63 years old and long past the time when he had wanted to retire. In his memo to himself 30 years earlier, he had promised to retire in two years. But his greed for money, his lust for power, and his desire to build the largest steel company in the world had put the date off time and again. In the 1890s he had been preoccupied with his labor troubles and the prolonged depression.

He was not the only partner in Carnegie Steel who had had enough. Frick wanted to cash in his holdings, move to New York, build a great art collection, and live a free life. Some of the other partners, too, wanted to enjoy their long-delayed millioniaredom. Their profits from the shares in the company had continually been invested and reinvested in new equipment and in unending expansion.

All would have been happy if they could have sold their shares at fair market value. But an "iron clad agreement" Carnegie had forced on them in 1887 built all sorts of barriers to that. The only possible way out, the partners agreed, was to find an outside buyer who would make Carnegie an offer he could not refuse. But who? There were few potential buyers with the capital needed to do that, for the firm had become the largest industrial unit in the world, employing 20,000 people.

Carnegie Steel, wrote one of Carnegie's biographers, Harold Livesay:

> bore his name and it had a mission in Carnegie's life. He . . . sought a haven of rest, but his business was the only vessel that could take him there. There was so much to make up for: the failure of his father; the ignominious flight from poverty; the people ground up and fed to his insatiable ambition—Woodruff, Kloman, Tom Scott, his own brother Tom; the lies to get contracts; the brutality to make them pay; the greed and trickery; and Homestead, always there was Homestead. But he could make up for it with all the wealth and power which his company, his "concern" as he often called it, could bring him. It was the instrument of atonement, clean and hard and pure as American steel and the fire that made it.

He could use it as "an instrument of atonement," but first he had to sell it. One of the possible buyers was J. P. Morgan. Like Carnegie, he was in his mid-sixties. If Carnegie was the king of steel, Morgan was the king of high finance. For years he had been building trusts, combines, and interlocking directorates that would eliminate the wasteful and destructive competitiveness. Recently he had become interested in steel and had himself created two steel companies. He saw Carnegie's furious undercutting of his competition in steel as a menace to his own interests and realized that the only way to stop him was to buy him out.

At a dinner in New York's University Club in December 1900, given to honor Charles Schwab, president of Carnegie Steel, Morgan was seated at Schwab's side. To the audience of 80 influential leaders of American finance

Powerful financier J. P. Morgan bought out Carnegie in 1900, making the poor boy from Scotland the richest man in the world.

and industry Schwab gave a talk outlining a future in which the whole steel industry could be organized as a sort of supertrust, with every plant playing its assigned part. Morgan was obviously Schwab's real target, and after the dinner Morgan said, let's get together to talk this over.

A few days later they met at Morgan's home, in a secret session that Carnegie knew nothing about. Morgan said he would be interested in buying Carnegie out. But was the man really ready to sell? Schwab then met privately with Louise Carnegie to ask her advice on how to broach this to her husband. She was eager to see Andrew quit the business and give all his attention to his philanthropic interests. Go play golf with him tomorrow, she said. He's always in a good mood at this new game he just started playing. The next day Schwab let Carnegie win easily and then, over lunch, told him of his talk with Morgan and that the banker, check in hand, was waiting for Carnegie's "Yes."

Carnegie thought it over that night, and the next morning, scribbling a few figures on a sheet of paper, handed it to Schwab and told him to see if Morgan would accept it. At the foot of the notes was the total price he was asking for the Carnegie company and all its holdings: $480 million. (Today that is the equivalent of about $12.5 billion.)

Down on Wall Street, Morgan took a quick look at the paper and said, "I accept this price." The biggest deal in American industrial history was done, that easily.

Morgan asked Carnegie to meet him at his home. The two spent 15 minutes talking. Then Morgan shook Carnegie's hand and said, "Mr. Carnegie, I want to congratulate you on being the richest man in the world."

THIRTEEN

THE ART
OF GIVING

Carnegie did not wait for retirement to begin spending some of his wealth on good works. As early as 1879 he had given his birthplace of Dunfermline its first public swimming pool. Two years later he gave it a free public library, and another library went to the town of Braddock, the site of one of his steel mills. The Swedenborgian church his father had attended was gifted with a pipe organ.

So rich a public figure as Carnegie was bombarded with requests for financial help. He refused most of them because he felt such giving was merely charity. In a two-part article called "Wealth" published in the *North American Review* in 1889, he explained his thinking about money and its best uses. He believed the accumulation of great wealth under the capitalist system was inevitable. He traced the evolution of modern society to the law of competition, "which may be sometimes hard for the individual." He admitted there was a great price to be paid under a rigid class system, with the employers forced into paying the lowest wages and frequent friction between capital and labor, between rich and poor.

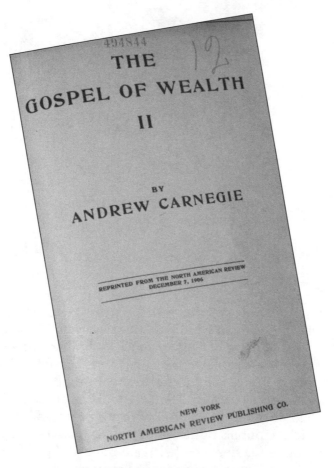

THE GOSPEL OF WEALTH II

BY
ANDREW CARNEGIE

REPRINTED FROM THE NORTH AMERICAN REVIEW
DECEMBER 7, 1906

NEW YORK
NORTH AMERICAN REVIEW PUBLISHING CO.

This essay by Carnegie on the art of giving raised great controversy.

But, he went on, the system is best for people, "because it insures the survival of the fittest in every department." You can't eliminate such individualism, he claimed, without first changing human nature.

Yet that system, though it invariably gives wealth only to the few, is nevertheless beneficial, he said. Provided, he added, that the amasser of wealth realizes that he or she is but a steward responsible for returning that fortune to the society out of which it came.

He then set about showing how the art of giving could be made into a science.

He listed seven areas in which "the wise trustees of surplus wealth should invest to benefit and advance the general welfare":

1. *Found a university.*
2. *Establish a free library.*
3. *Found at least one hospital, medical school, laboratory, or other institution devoted to alleviating human suffering.*
4. *Establish a public park.*
5. *Build halls suitable for musical concerts and meetings of all kinds.*
6. *Build public swimming pools.*
7. *Provide permanent structures for churches.*

Not all wealthy people will agree on these avenues for expending surplus wealth, he pointed out. Each should consider what appeals to his or her own interest. Nor should millionaires alone work for measures to benefit the community. Everyone who has but a small surplus above his moderate needs may use it to such ends. And those without any surplus can volunteer at least part of their time to community service. That is "usually as important as funds, and often more so."

With the appearance of Carnegie's "Gospel According to St. Andrew," as some derisively labeled the article, a hail of criticism descended upon him. His basic assumption of the inevitability of great wealth was attacked by William J. Tucker, a professor of religion. Tucker asserted there was nothing inevitable about becoming a multimillionaire, nor was it consistent with democracy or justice. Tucker did not believe the man sitting atop his mountain of moneybags was necessarily the best administrator of its redistribution. "I can conceive of no greater mistake," he said, "than that of trying to make charity do the work of justice."

Tucker may have been striking at the heart of Carnegie's own motive for philanthropy. Carnegie himself wrote that the very rich should avoid extravagant living so that "they can, perhaps, also find refuge from self-questioning in the thought of the much greater portion of their means which is being spent upon others." In Carnegie's 1868 memo to himself, he said that to concentrate "most of my thoughts wholly upon the way to make more money in the shortest time must degrade me beyond hope of permanent recovery." Nevertheless he continued at ever faster speed to do exactly that—make more and more money.

In his autobiography (1920) Carnegie gave relatively little space to his philanthropies. Such critics as Tucker upset him but did not change his views. One of his first actions upon retirement was to set up the Andrew Carnegie Relief Fund to provide financial assistance to his former employees in need. It helped those injured in accidents and provided small pensions for those needing help in old age. Doing this, said his relentless critics, enabled him to tell the public how much he loved his workers and that they still loved him, in spite of Homestead.

He endowed the Carnegie Institute of his adopted Pittsburgh, starting it as a library, then developing it into an enormous building covering four acres that also housed an art gallery, a natural history museum, and a music hall. Under the institute's direction technical schools were created that later became the Carnegie Institute of Technology, also handsomely endowed.

The working people's own cultural activities in a city like Pittsburgh offended the rich and respectable. In Pittsburgh the immigrant working-class neighborhoods enjoyed theater, sports, and clubs as well as networks of tobacco shops, groceries, and small stores where information and gossip were exchanged. But the ruling elite did not like the "low" sensational and commercial pastimes of the working class. So when Carnegie opened his Pittsburgh museum, library, and music hall in 1895, he promoted high culture for the masses. The music hall offered free Sunday organ recitals "to develop the musical instincts of the people" by refusing to play "all music of low or vulgar character." So important was music to Carnegie that he provided funding for eight thousand pipe organs in churches and synagogues wherever they aroused his interest.

Carnegie gave generously to technology and science

Carnegie's private study in his Fifth Avenue home

because of the lessons he learned from seeing the great contributions to his own enterprises by young apprentices who made themselves into inventors and technologists. Well-endowed technical and scientific institutions would give such talented young people a great opportunity to contribute to social as well as industrial advance.

Quite different was Carnegie's Hero Fund, which he created in 1904. He proudly asserted that it was his own idea to use his gift of $5 million to reward heroes or to support the families of heroes "who perish in the effort to serve or save their fellows." Later he extended the fund to Great Britain and other countries of Europe. By 1995 the fund had honored some 7,500 North Americans.

Early in his philanthropic projects he insisted on being consulted on everything from the architectural design to the most minute choice of the art to adorn both the interior and exterior of a building. But because he was giving on so huge a scale this soon became too demanding a task. He then figured out ways to make his philanthropy as efficient and standardized as his steel mills.

He made sure he was present and spoke at the openings of as many of his projects as possible. He loved doing it, yet claimed he put himself out only to set an example of what other wealthy men might do. But these frequent and dramatic public displays, always featured handsomely in the press, only entrenched the belief of many that he was an incurable publicity hound. Poultney Bigelow, a man who worked with him on development of the New York Public Library system, wrote acidly of Carnegie:

> *Never before in the history of plutocratic America had any one man purchased by mere money so much social advertising and flattery. No wonder that he felt himself infallible, when Lords temporal and spiritual courted him and hung upon his words. They wanted his money, and flattery alone would wring it from him. Ask him for aid in a small deserv-*

ing case or to assist a struggling scientific explorer—that would be wasted time. He had no ears for any charity unless labeled with his name. He would have given millions to Greece had she labeled the Parthenon "Carnegopolis."

A close examination of Carnegie's larger philanthropic projects shows that his major focus was on education. More than 80 percent of his fortune went in that direction—to libraries, colleges and universities, institutions for scientific research and the spreading of knowledge, and individual grants and pensions to college teachers.

Let's look at his gifts to libraries. That field is what is closest to most of us. Millions upon millions of people have entered the doors of Carnegie libraries almost everywhere in America, to read books, newspapers, and magazines; to look up material needed for school studies; to prepare for professional qualifying exams; or to satisfy dozens of other needs.

Carnegie always said he wanted to help only those people who could help themselves. He tested that capacity in communities requesting libraries by providing the money to erect the building. But the community had to guarantee to stock it with books, to maintain it, and to pay the salaries of staff. He was saying, don't throw away money on someone lacking the strength of character to make the best use of it. The fact that he and other wealthy people had made lots of money seemed to him proof of their intellectual and moral superiority. It was only natural for them to act as the stewards of their wealth for the good of the community.

Remember how his passion for libraries began when as a working boy he was given access to Colonel James Anderson's private library in Allegheny. This experience made this weaver's son interested in helping other poor boys use libraries to pull themselves up the ladder of commercial success. So he began his philanthropic career by offering libraries to towns he was personally connected with: a library in Dunfermline in 1881, and five years later, another in Allegheny City, his first home in the United States. Soon after, he gave libraries to Pittsburgh, Johnstown, Braddock, and Homestead, sites of his homes or steelworks.

In the Allegheny library a large portrait of Carnegie hung above the mantel of the massive fireplace that dominated the central room. It made library users "look upon Carnegie as a rich uncle," said one historian, "who deserved respect, obedience, and affection, and whose affection in return precluded any class resentment."

Articles began appearing in the press questioning the moral dimensions of accepting philanthropic gifts. A congregational minister, Washington Gladden of Ohio, wrote that if you accepted money earned by illegal or unethical means, you "condoned the wrongs by which [such funds] were obtained." Gladden was the first to attack philanthropic paternalism and to label such gifts tainted money. He was voicing the distrust of big business that was common in the Populist movement and in the muckraking press. A direct poke at Carnegie was made by the humorist Finley Peter Dunne when he had his fictitious Irishman Mr. Dooley say, "The way to abolish poverty an' bust crime is to put up a brownstone buildin' in ivry town in the country with me name over it."

Rather than halt the gifts to libraries, Carnegie increased them. By 1917 nearly 1,700 libraries were promised in more than 1,400 towns. To ease the burden of overseeing the projects, he reformed his system of philanthropy. Carnegie structured the entire enterprise in the form of a corporation, one dedicated not to making money but to giving it away. He centralized decision making and regularized mistakes. The new organization, called the Carnegie Corporation, was one of the first modern foundations. It was founded in 1911, with an initial endowment of $120 million.

Carnegie's gift of thousands of free public libraries is seen by a cartoonist as a means of cementing his fame.

Carnegie libraries provided the first library experience for many thousands of young readers in the first part of the 20th century. Children and especially immigrant children were regular and frequent library users. Like the settlement houses of the urban neighborhoods, the library helped them absorb American culture.

Librarians reported that immigrant children relished the chance to spend an afternoon in a warm, clean, safe, sunlit setting where they could breathe fresh air. Often the appeal was not that the library was quiet, for many times it

SOCIAL DARWINISM

Carnegie's ideas about wealth were taken in part from a system of thought called social Darwinism. It was a misinterpretation of Charles Darwin's *The Origin of Species* (1859). In that famous book Darwin concluded that plant and animal species had evolved through a process of natural selection. In the struggle for existence, some species managed to adapt to their environment and survive. Those that failed to adapt perished.

Herbert Spencer, an English social philosopher and friend of Carnegie's, seized on the idea of the survival of the fittest and applied it to human society—which Darwin had never done. Spencer's theory attributed the amassing of great wealth to men of "superior ability, foresight and adaptability." Don't mess with the economic world, he warned, because such interference would tamper with the natural laws of selection.

Spencer's American followers, including leading men of business, science, religion, and politics, promoted the basic ideas of social Darwinism. Poverty in any society, they held, is the inevitable consequence of the struggle for existence. To try to end poverty is not only pointless but immoral.

Upholders of social Darwinism often believed in the superiority of whites, particularly Anglo-Saxons who, they claimed, had attained the highest stage of evolution. That notion was used to justify racism and imperialism.

Carnegie at times ignored some of Spencer's ideas and even ran directly against them. Carnegie favored providing for the general welfare through legislative action. The only way to gain the eight-hour day, he insisted, was through federal legislation. Union negotiations would not achieve the goal because most employers were too strongly against it. "Whatever experience shows that the State can do best I am in favor of the State doing," he said.

And while Spencer thought philanthropy only did harm by interfering with the law of the survival of the fittest, Carnegie believed in the social responsibility of the wealthy. Eventually, wrote Carnegie's biographer, Joseph Wall, "Carnegie was to abandon even the pretense" of accepting Spencer's brand of social Darwinism.

was not, but that it was heated in the fall and winter. One grown-up remembered going to the library in the South Bronx because it was "a refuge and a sanctuary," a place to go "when things got rough or when somebody was after me—which was often."

After 1917 no new Carnegie library grants were made. Rising wartime costs of construction and the shortage of professionally trained librarians accounted in part for that decision. About 1925 the Carnegie Corporation began a new program of library support, offering grants to the American Library Association, to library training schools, and to academic libraries.

Despite the criticism he suffered for his philanthropy, Carnegie drew his greatest satisfaction from what his library program accomplished. Was any other gift so popular? Did any have so strong an influence on so large a number of people? Almost nowhere in America before 1880 could you find a public library. It was his gifts that made the library as vital a part of America as the schoolhouse. Only a generation after he launched the library program, about 35 million people a day were making use of his libraries. Those libraries are his strongest claim to popular fame.

EDUCATION
AND PEACE

In 1902 the Carnegies moved into their home at Fifth Avenue and 91st Street in Manhattan. Located at least 20 blocks north of the shops, hotels, and grand mansions of the rich, the site was promptly labeled Carnegie Hill.

Carnegie had his architects design an immense mansion that took four years to build and cost $1.5 million. It was built of red brick in classic Georgian style. Around it was a large garden. The home contained seven stories, three below ground level and four above. The 64 rooms incorporated all the latest innovations in heating, cooling, lighting, and sanitation. The first floor held Carnegie's library-study. Carved into its wood paneling were noble slogans that had inspired him as he climbed ever onward and upward. (Today the building houses the Cooper-Hewitt National Design Museum.)

In 1897, at the time he commissioned the design of his Fifth Avenue home, Carnegie and his wife, Louise, had their only child, named Margaret after his mother. About that time they decided they must have their own summer home in Scotland, instead of always renting one. They

The Carnegie home on New York's Fifth Avenue at 91st Street. The family moved into it in 1902. It now houses the Cooper-Hewitt National Design Museum.

wanted a place with a view of the sea, a waterfall, and a trout stream. They settled on an ancient estate called Skibo, which had a ruined old castle, thousands of acres of moors, and a view of the sea in the distance, but no waterfall.

Carnegie bought more land, eventually extending the estate to 32,000 acres, built a new baronial castle, and created a waterfall. It was ready for use in 1902. He hired a staff of 85 to take care of the needs of the family and the many and frequent guests. The Carnegies spent five months of every year there, with fishing, hunting, swimming, yachting, and golf to entertain their guests.

After seven seasons at Skibo, they realized they needed a rest from constantly entertaining guests, and each year began to spend three weeks by themselves in a small stone cottage on the moors. Their young daughter, Margaret,

Skibo Castle, the summer home Carnegie built in the Scottish Highlands.

early on showed a streak of the radicalism of her Dunfermline forbears. She would ask her parents, "Why do we invite rich people and give them everything when they have plenty at home? And the poor haven't?" Carnegie remarked about such questions, "Already the young socialist crops out. . . . Questions easier to ask than to answer."

When Carnegie had first begun to provide grants for educational purposes there had been much speculation about who and what would get the funding. Would he enrich a select few, like the Ivy League schools? Or found a great new university, like Stanford, named for its benefactor? But only slowly, reluctantly, did he fund the Carnegie Institute of Technology (now Carnegie-Mellon University) in Pittsburgh. Most of his institutional gifts went to small colleges with small endowments. The only schools that got larger gifts were Hampton and Tuskegee, which drew black students from the rural South, and Berea, whose white students came from the mountains of Kentucky. In these three schools the students worked on campus to put themselves through college, where they learned useful crafts and trades. Perhaps these gifts were influenced by Carnegie's early experiences in growing up poor.

Yet Carnegie had a greater impact on higher education than anyone expected when he became aware of what small salaries college professors earned even at well-endowed schools. He was shocked in 1890, when he found that professors with decades of teaching experience were rarely paid more than $400 a year and received nothing in the way of pensions for retirement.

While visiting Carnegie, the head of Massachusetts Institute of Technology pointed out that an engineer earned three to five times as much as a professor of engineering. How could MIT find the best people for its faculty under so inequitable a system? And with no pension plan for professors, a university often kept teachers long past retirement age, a fact that discouraged young people from going into teaching.

These insights moved Carnegie to action. In 1905 he launched the Carnegie Teachers Pension Fund. But he did not want his money to go to just any applicant. He also set up the Carnegie Foundation for the Advancement of Teaching, which devised standards for admission to the pension fund. The standards were set so high that a great majority of the applicants were rejected. The unforeseen, unplanned effect was to advance the standards of higher education more than any other program might have done.

By 1909 the Carnegie Foundation had become the national unofficial accrediting agency for colleges and universities.

With the number of eligible faculty becoming ever larger, a free pension fund proved impossible to sustain. So in 1917 an independent legal reserve life insurance company was chartered, called the Teachers Insurance and Annuity Association of America. The Carnegie Corporation funded its initial capital and surplus to get it started, and by 1938 TIAA was able to become a totally independent nonprofit insurance company.

No matter how hard Carnegie worked at giving away money, he could not empty the seemingly bottomless bucket. The interest he drew from his bonds kept outpacing the spending of that money. After ten years during which he gave away about $180 million he still had almost the same sum left. He told Elihu Root, a lawyer friend, that if he could not get rid of all his wealth in the short time left to him, he would die in disgrace.

That was how the Carnegie Corporation was born in 1911. The lawyer proposed setting up a trust and transferring the bulk of Carnegie's fortune into it for others to worry about. And then you'll die happy, he said, in a state of grace. Carnegie became the president of the corporation and the presidents of all his other philanthropic institutions joined the board of trustees. It was the first supertrust in the history of philanthropy. The corporation's capital fund, originally donated at a value of about $135 million, had a market value of $1.2 billion by the end of 1995. In 1996 the corporation allotted $59 million for grants. The three major programs for its grants are:

1. *Education and Health Development of Children and Youth*
2. *Preventing Deadly Conflict*
3. *Strengthening Human Resources in Developing Countries.*

The Carnegie Library and Music Hall in Pittsburgh opened in 1895.

In the last stage of his life Carnegie gave most of his energy to the cause of peace. He had long advocated international arbitration when disputes arose among nations. His program for world peace called for frequent meetings among the heads of states of the great powers. He wanted to submit all disputes between nations to an international tribunal or court for settlement. To enforce that tribunal's decisions a League of Peace should be empowered to impose economic sanctions. If such measures failed, an international police force should compel the aggressor nation to obey the decisions.

In a speech to a Peace Society in London in 1910 Carnegie said:

Surely no civilized community in our day can resist the conclusion that the killing of man by man, as a means of settling international disputes, is the foulest blot upon human society, the greatest curse of human life, and as long as men continue thus to kill one another they have slight claim to rank as civilized, since in this respect they remain savages.

In the pursuit of peace Carnegie spent money lavishly. He built three imposing "temples of peace" and endowed four major peace foundations, among them the Carnegie Endowment for International Peace. Never content to be only a fountain of cash, he also wanted to exert leadership in the struggle against war. His writing and speeches in the early 1900s were devoted to the cause of peace.

Although he was never secretary of state to any president, he assumed the unofficial role of secretary of peace. No president liked it, but they could not stem the tide of letters and telegrams and personal visits designed to show them the true way to international peace. So, too, did he offer unsolicited advice to monarchs, prime ministers, foreign secretaries, and ambassadors everywhere war threatened.

How a cartoonist predicted Carnegie would look after he gave away all his money.

He hammered constantly at his key policy: face-to-face summit meetings between heads of nations to resolve their conflicts peacefully. Like many peace advocates, Carnegie showed a strong faith in treaties and international agreements. He believed in this, despite his long experience in the business world where agreements were made almost every day and then broken just as easily when it suited someone's interests. The sincerity of Carnegie's desire to end war is unquestionable, but he had a naïve optimism in the ability of pacifists to bring it about by getting a few heads of state to talk things over.

Twice Carnegie met with Kaiser Wilhelm, in 1907 and again in 1912, because he believed the German emperor was the key figure in bringing about peace among the great powers. But scarcely two years after their last consultation, the guns of World War I boomed, and German armies swept through Belgium toward Paris.

Carnegie's hopes for peace had failed. "The world disaster was too much" for him, Carnegie's wife wrote. "His heart was broken."

A COMMENTATOR
ON EVERYTHING

Among all the titans of industry in his time Carnegie stood out for one unique quality. While the others achieved dominance in their fields, amassed great wealth, and gave handsomely to philanthropic causes, none aspired to the additional role that Carnegie took on.

Why talk about what you were doing as you gathered all that power and made all that money? Wasn't it safer and smarter to keep quiet, to hug your secrets close, and let the competition and your critics only guess?

This was not the way Carnegie saw it. He made himself a commentator on capitalism, on democracy, on education, on population, on socialism, on war, on race relations, on peace, on everything. At times there seemed no limit to what caught his fancy. With voice and pen he told everyone what he thought about everything. He always kept his tongue well oiled and his pen at the ready.

At age 17 he had made his debut in print with a letter to the editor about Colonel Anderson's library. Over the next 40 years, while building and managing his vast industrial empire, he somehow found the time and energy to

Carnegie at his desk, where he wrote his books, articles, and speeches.

write eight books and 64 articles, and had 10 of his major speeches published in pamphlet form. After his retirement from the steel business in 1901, he continued to write, speak, and publish.

The articles were not confined to small audiences reading specialized journals. Most of them appeared in the highest quality magazines read by the general educated public in the United States and Great Britain. His work was welcomed by editors because it sold so well. He wrote simply and clearly and was able to make complex subjects easily understood. His writings were rich in personal anecdote and in aphorisms. Above all, his own spirit of optimism pervaded his writings. Reading or listening to him made audiences feel good. He did not hesitate to bring up controversial issues. Whether or not his readers agreed with what he said, they enjoyed his pungent way of saying it.

Readers of today, accustomed to the fact that ghost-writers are almost always behind the words attributed to presidents, corporate chiefs, or even celebrity novelists and autobiographers, may think Carnegie did not write his own speeches, articles, or books. But researchers studying his manuscripts are confident that he alone was responsible for all that he produced.

One of Carnegie's most popular books was *Triumphant Democracy* (1886). It was a kind of Fourth of July oration, voicing his belief in the great value of material progress and in America's mission to set an example of democracy for the rest of the world. But the book was more than a sermon in praise of democracy. It was also a defense of America's individualistic business system. And more than that, it expressed Carnegie's need to reconcile his radical Scottish past with his plutocratic present.

Always conscious of his handicap of having only a few years of elementary schooling in Dunfermline, Carnegie persistently pursued the acquisition of culture. Early on, when he moved to New York, he joined the Nineteenth Century Club and took part in readings of assigned papers. At the club he met people of widely differing views and discussed with them economics, politics, literature, and religion. Thus, he came to know many of America's leading thinkers. He met such writers as George Washington Cable, Thomas W. Higginson, and Julia Ward Howe; political fig-

A caricature by Cesare of Mark Twain teasing his friend Andrew Carnegie at a dinner in "Saint Andrew's" honor in 1907.

ures such as Theodore Roosevelt; and purveyors of public opinion like John Swinton, the chief of the *New York Times* editorial staff. He also got to know distinguished clergy of the Catholic, Protestant, and Jewish faiths, as well as the freethinker Robert G. Ingersoll. These acquaintances led him to friendships with such influential British thinkers as Herbert Spencer, Matthew Arnold, William E. Gladstone, and Charles Kingsley. John Morley, the British statesmen, became his closest friend.

By now Carnegie was a polished man of the world. His wealth, power, and international eminence made it possible for him to meet anyone, however important, and talk with them as an equal. Speaking to crowds, of course, was different. He was not a natural orator. His voice was high-pitched and not pleasing to the ear. But on the public platform he made up for it by playing the dramatic showman. Because he was so short, he needed to stretch himself as tall as possible for the audience to see him above the lectern. "Frequently rising to his tiptoes," an observer said, "and pumping his short arms vigorously, to his critics in the audience he looked like a bantam rooster ready to crow."

He had first practiced making speeches as a boy in Pittsburgh, forming a debating club with his young friends. Later he gave this advice:

My two rules for speaking then (and now) were: Make yourself perfectly at home before your audience, and simply talk to them, not at them. Do not try to be somebody else: be your own self and talk, never "orate" until you can't help it.

His views were confirmed when he asked Colonel Ingersoll, one of the most popular speakers of the time, to what he attributed his powers. "Avoid elocutionists like the snakes," he said, "and be yourself." Carnegie's natural humor helped considerably. His talks were often interrupted by laughter and applause. He was also a master of impromptu speaking. He could give off-the-cuff remarks that delighted his listeners.

Rather than invite business leaders or the social elite into his home, Carnegie much preferred the company of men like Spencer, Morley, Arnold, Rudyard Kipling, Oliver Wendell Holmes, and Mark Twain. He liked to socialize with people whose minds were more interesting than their bank balance. Twain was often Carnegie's dinner companion. The steel king sent him bottles, cases, and finally even barrels of his favorite private-stock whisky. "Whisky never comes at the wrong time," Twain responded to one of many such gifts.

From the time Twain first met Carnegie in the 1890s, he found the little Scottish steelmaster a fascinating study of the "Human Being Unconcealed." The multimillionaire

counted Twain one of the most glittering prizes in the
Carnegie collection of celebrities and often was generous
with him. "For the sake of the future centuries," Twain put
down these impressions of Carnegie:

> *He has bought fame and paid cash for it; he has deliberately
> projected and planned out this fame for himself; he has
> arranged that his name shall be famous in the mouths of
> men for centuries to come. He has planned shrewdly, safely,
> securely, and will have his desire. Any town or village or
> hamlet on the globe can have a public library upon these fol-
> lowing unvarying terms; when the applicant shall have
> raised one-half of the necessary money, Carnegie will fur-
> nish the other half, and the library building must perma-
> nently bear his name.*

> *I think that three or four centuries from now Carnegie
> libraries will be considerably thicker in the world than
> churches. It is a long-headed idea and will deceive many
> people into thinking Carnegie a long-headed man in many
> and many a wise small way—the way of the trimmer, the
> way of the smart calculator, the way that enables a man to
> correctly calculate the tides and come in with the flow and
> go out with the ebb, keeping a permanent place on the top of
> the wave of advantage while other men as intelligent as he,
> but more addicted to principle and less to policy, get strand-
> ed on the reefs and bars.*

> *He has never a word of brag about his real achievements;
> they do not seen to interest him in the least degree; he is
> only interested—and intensely interested—in the flatteries
> lavished upon him in the disguise of compliments and in
> other little vanities which other men would value but con-
> ceal. I must repeat he is an astonishing man in his genuine
> modesty as regards the large things he has done, and in his
> juvenile delight in trivialities that feed his vanity.*

Mr. Carnegie is not any better acquainted with himself than if he had met himself for the first time day before yesterday. He thinks he is a rude, bluff, independent spirit, who writes his mind and thinks his mind with an almost extravagant Fourth of July independence; whereas he is really the counterpart of the rest of the human race in that he does not boldly speak his mind except when there isn't any danger in it. He thinks he is a scorner of kings and emperors and dukes, whereas he is like the rest of the human race; a slight attention from one of these can make him drunk for a week and keep his happy tongue wagging for seven years.

When America's war with Spain began in 1898, Carnegie and Twain had both supported it as an effort to free Cuba. But early in 1900, with the United States now fighting in the Philippines, Twain came to feel, as he told the press, that "we do not intend to free but to subjugate the people. We have gone there to conquer not to redeem. It should, it seems to me, be our pleasure and duty to make those people free and let them deal with their own domestic questions in their own way. And so I am an anti-imperialist. I am opposed to having the eagle put its talons on any other land."

Both Carnegie and Twain became active in the Anti-Imperialist League, an organization a great many writers joined, as did some leading Democrats, Republicans, and other public figures. Twain wrote a scorching indictment of American foreign policy in the *North American Review* (which often published Carnegie too) called "To the Person Sitting in Darkness." When it appeared in February 1900, Carnegie put up $1,000 to reprint the piece as a pamphlet to be distributed by the Anti-Imperialist League— "the only missionary work," said Carnegie, "I am responsible for."

When Carnegie's retirement was announced, he got a note from Twain. All the papers were commenting on the huge sum J. P. Morgan had paid to acquire Carnegie Steel. Twain wrote:

Dear Sir and Friend:

You seem to be prosperous these days. Could you lend an admirer a dollar and a half to buy a hymn-book with? God will bless you if you do; I feel it, I know it. So will I. If there should be other applications this one not to count.

Yours,

Mark

P.S. Don't send the hymn-book, send the money. I want to make the selection myself.

Carnegie, enjoying his friend's humor, reprinted the note in his autobiography.

The Carnegies were at their retreat at Skibo in August 1914 when news came that the Great War had begun. Britain, France, and Russia were at war with Germany and Austria-Hungary. Carnegie had just finished writing his autobiography, a book "all sunshine, sunshine, sunshine." And then the terrible news broke into his last page. He added, "What a change! The world convulsed by war as never before! I dare not relinquish all hope."

Louise Carnegie said that never again was he able to interest himself in private affairs. He tried to write now and then, but found it useless. "The world disaster was too much," his wife said. His long quest for peace had come to nothing. Visitors still turned up at Skibo, but in mid-September, six weeks before the usual departure time, Carnegie realized it was their final farewell. As he crossed

Carnegie poses with his collie at his Skibo estate.

the Atlantic on the way home, he wrote to Woodrow Wilson, suggesting the president call the warring nations together and act as arbitrator to seek a settlement and silence the guns. It was far too late for that.

In early 1915, at age 80, Carnegie caught pneumonia and was seriously ill for six weeks. His physical recovery was complete, but his spirit seemed shattered. He sank into a deep depression. As the war raged over Europe, the killing mounted into the millions. Its horror was too much for him to bear.

Unable to return to Skibo, in 1916 the Carnegies bought a large stone mansion near Lenox, Massachusetts, called Shadowbrook. It sat on a high hill overlooking a lake, and surrounding it were the lovely Berkshire Hills. It was the next best thing to Skibo for natural beauty. By the spring of 1917 Germany and the United States were close to war. Carnegie believed the only way to gain world peace was for America to enter the war and help the Allies defeat Germany. He had moved from pacifism to militarism while his English friend John Morley clung to the principle that all war was criminal folly.

When the United States entered the war in April 1917 Carnegie bought Liberty Bonds in support of the government. The business world no longer interested him. He was only interested in the means of conducting the war and winning it. At Shadowbrook that summer he took long motor trips in the countryside and went fishing and boating in the lake, but he felt lonely without the swarm of friends who used to keep him company at Skibo. When the war ended in November 1918 he was excited by Wilson's proposal for a League of Nations to prevent other wars, a notion he had himself offered several years earlier. He reached his 83rd birthday in November 1918, and soon after his daughter, Margaret, married a young ensign, Roswell Miller, the son of a former railroad president.

Though they had planned to go back to Skibo castle that summer of 1919, it was plain that Carnegie, now a feeble old man, a venerable relic of a fast-disappearing era, was in no condition to make the ocean voyage. When Louise told him they had better not go now but surely would go next year, he looked at her and said, "There won't be a next year for me." So they started the summer at Shadowbrook. Again Carnegie came down with pneumonia. He was so frail and dispirited he seemed to welcome his end. Early in the morning on August 11, 1919, he died.

As he had requested, he was buried in the Sleepy Hollow Cemetery at North Tarrytown, New York. His grave, marked by a Celtic cross cut from stone quarried near Skibo, carried these words:

Andrew Carnegie

Born in Dunfermline, Scotland, 25 November 1835

Died in Lenox, Massachusetts, 11 August 1919

A NOTE ON SOURCES

Andrew Carnegie loved to talk and write. His speeches, letters, articles, and books convey a sense of his remarkable personality—as he saw himself and as he wished others to see him. His drive for success, his lust for wealth, his pleasure in power, and his enjoyment of privilege and celebrity come through in his own words, as does his self-imposed duty to give away nearly all his gigantic fortune. Much of what he wrote demonstrates his struggle to live by his youthful radical convictions in the face of a business career that subjected them to enormous pressures.

PRIMARY SOURCES

The major collections of Carnegie's papers are housed in the manuscript divisions of the New York Public Library and the Library of Congress in Washington, D.C.

His *Autobiography*, first published in 1920, is now available in a Northeastern University Press edition, 1986. The man's flavor is enjoyable, but he omits some elements of his experience and distorts others so that he always makes himself look good.

The *Andrew Carnegie Reader*, edited and with excellent introductory notes by Carnegie's biographer Joseph Frazier Wall, was published by the University of Pittsburgh Press in 1992. It includes 26 selections from speeches, articles, and books, reflecting several aspects of Carnegie's life.

Earlier, in 1968, Burton J. Hendrick edited *Andrew Carnegie: Miscellaneous Writings*, in a two-volume edition for the Book of the Libraries Press. Of the eight books Carnegie wrote, the more significant are *Triumphant Democracy*, (New York: Scribner's, 1886), *The Gospel of Wealth*, (New York: Century, 1900), and *The Empire of Business*, (Westport, CT: Greenwood, 1968). His other titles include several reporting on his travels abroad.

SECONDARY SOURCES

The best and most comprehensive biography—one unlikely to be replaced soon—is by Joseph Frazier Wall: *Andrew Carnegie*, 1970, reissued by the University of Pittsburgh Press in 1989. It runs to 1,137 pages, but there is hardly a dull paragraph and everything helps explain the man and his times.

A much briefer treatment is Harold C. Livesay's *Andrew Carnegie and the Rise of Big Business* (New York: HarperCollins, 1975). Its emphasis obviously is on the man's role in creating his steel empire. The same focus shapes Louis M. Hacker's *The World of Andrew Carnegie, 1865–1901* (New York: Lippincott, 1968). *The Carnegie Nobody Knows*, by George Swetnam and Helene Smith (McDonald, 1989), discloses no secrets but is nevertheless useful. A brilliant essay, "Andrew Carnegie," by the historian Robert Heilbroner, appeared in *American Heritage* magazine in August 1960 and is collected in the American Heritage reader called *A Sense of History* (New York: Smithmark, 1996).

One of the most famous industrial conflicts in history was the strike and lockout at Carnegie's Homestead steel plant in 1892. Two books are the product of long and intensive research into the forces that shaped the defining battle between management and organized labor. Both studies are enormously rich in detail. Paul Krause's *The Battle for Homestead, 1880–1892: Politics, Culture and Steel*, was issued by University of Pittsburgh Press in 1992. That same year Times Books published William Serrin's *Homestead: The Glory and Tragedy of an American Steel Town*. The truth about Carnegie's personal responsibility for what happened at Homestead is documented in both books. In Samuel Yellen's *American Labor Struggles* (New York: Harcourt, 1936), and in Milton Meltzer's *Bread and Roses: The Struggle of American Labor, 1865–1915* (New York: Knopf, 1967, reissued by Facts on File, 1991), there are chapters on Homestead.

Background on labor history of the period may be found in David Brody, *Steel Workers in America: the Non-Union Era*, (Cambridge, MA: Harvard University Press, 1960); *Workers' Struggles, Past and Present*, James Green, ed., (Philadelphia: Temple University Press, 1983); Joseph G. Rayback, *A History of American Labor* (New York: Free Press, 1966); Herbert G. Gutman, *Work, Culture and Society in Industrializing America* (New York: Knopf, 1976); and Thomas R. Brooks, *Toil and Trouble: A History of American Labor* (New York: Dutton, 1971).

For facts and insights into the developing American economy of the 19th century I found the following especially helpful: Stuart Pruchy, *Enterprise: The Dynamic Economy of a Free People* (Cambridge, MA: Harvard University Press, 1990); Walter Licht, *Industrializing America: The 19th Century* (Baltimore: Johns Hopkins University Press, 1995); Robert B. Gordon, *American Iron, 1607–1900* (Baltimore: Johns Hopkins University Press, 1996); Albro Martin, *Railroads Triumphant* (New York: Oxford University Press, 1992); and Matthew Josephson,

The Robber Barons: The Great American Capitalists 1861–1901 (New York: Harcourt Brace, 1934). For a clear picture of the interesting activities and structure of the Carnegie Corporation of New York I used its 1995 annual report.

A comprehensive study of one of Carnegie's major philanthropies, the libraries, is found in Abigail A. Van Slyck, *Free to All: Carnegie Libraries and American Culture, 1890–1920* (Chicago: University of Chicago Press, 1995).

Social Darwinism, a major current in the thought of Carnegie's time, is essential to an understanding of the period. It is canvassed in Richard Hofstadter, *Social Darwinism in American Thought*, rev. ed. (New York: Braziller, 1959).

Carnegie's application of the newest science and technology to his production enterprises can be seen through two books that cover the field. They are A. Hunter Dupree, *Science and the Emergence of Modern America, 1865–1916*, (New York: Rand McNally, 1963) and Mitchell Wilson, *American Science and Invention* (New York: Simon & Schuster, 1954).

Several of the major figures in Carnegies life are covered in autobiography or biography. These include Thomas A. Scott, Alexander L. Holley, Henry Clay Frick, Charles M. Schwab, J. P. Morgan, Herbert Spencer, John Morley, and Mark Twain.

INDEX